EVA'S STORY

A Story of **Triumph** with **EVA SCHLOSS**

Eva Schloss

EVA'S STORY

A survivor's tale
by the stepsister of Anne Frank

Eva Schloss

with
Evelyn Julia Kent

William B. Eerdmans Publishing Company

Grand Rapids, Michigan

AUTHOR'S NOTE

This is a true story. As it is told from memory,
some of the incidental detail may not always be quite accurate.

Eerdmans Books for Young Readers
Grand Rapids, Michigan
www.eerdmans.com

© 1988, 2010 Eva Schloss and Evelyn Julia Kent
All rights reserved

First published 1988 in Great Britain by W. H. Allen & Company
This edition published 2019 in the United States of America

Printed in the United States of America

27 26 25 24 23 22 21 20 19   1 2 3 4 5 6 7 8 9

**A catalog record of this book is available
from the Library of Congress.**

*This edition is dedicated to
my beloved mother
Fritzi Frank (1905–1998)
whose love, strength, and example
gave me back the confidence to lead a full life.*

Also

*To my daughters Caroline, Jacky, and Sylvia,
and to my father Erich and my brother Heinz,
whom they never knew,
with the hope that this book
will bring them closer.*

In every ghetto, in every deportation train, in every labour camp, even in the death camps, the will to resist was strong and took many forms; fighting with those few weapons that could be found, fighting with sticks and knives, individual acts of defiance and protest, the courage of obtaining food under the threat of death, the nobility of refusing to allow the Germans their final wish to gloat over panic and despair. Even passivity was a form of resistance. "Not to act," Emanuel Ringelblum wrote in the aftermath of one particularly savage reprisal, "not to lift a hand against the Germans, has become the quiet passive heroism of the common Jew." To die with dignity was a form of resistance. To resist the dehumanizing, brutalizing force of evil, to refuse to be abased to the level of animals, to live through the torment, to outlive the tormentors, these too were resistance. Merely to give witness by one's own testimony was, in the end, to contribute to a moral victory. Simply to survive was a victory of the human spirit.

MARTIN GILBERT
The Holocaust: A Jewish Tragedy
(Collins, 1986)

Contents

Contents

PART III
Journey through Russia

Acknowledgments

We could not have written this book without the interest and encouragement of many relatives and friends. However, we have to give special thanks to Zvi Schloss for his patient support and helpful advice; to Michael Davies for his erudite research into the chronology of the events of World War II against which the story is set; to Alistair McGechie for his able and sympathetic editing; to Pat Healy for her faith that this book would be published.

We owe much to Frank Entwistle whose constructive suggestions and wise counselling smoothed our way.

And finally to Fritzi Frank our love and grateful thanks for the copious notes and reminders that she gave without reservation.

Preface

This book started about three years ago. My husband and I were having coffee with our good friends Anita and Barry. Anita, who came to England as a child refugee in the 1930s, mentioned that her husband, who was ten years old when the war ended, did not really know anything about what had happened to me during the Holocaust.

After a few moments of hesitation, I slowly started to recount some of my experiences. Their questions were so keen, their interest so deep and yet their knowledge of those times appeared so small, that I found myself going into details, some of which I had not revealed to anyone before and had, in fact, suppressed for many years.

At the end of the evening we were all in tears and almost speechless with emotion. My friends were shocked at the thought of how remote most people now are from those events.

They — and my husband — urged me to write my story. This thought pursued me in the weeks that followed. It gave rise to others: I let my life pass in front of me. In spite of what had happened to me during the war I have no feelings of bitterness or hate, but on the other hand I do not believe in the goodness of man.

My posthumous step-sister, Anne Frank, wrote in her *Diary:* "I still believe that deep down human beings are good at heart." I cannot help remembering that she wrote this *before* she experienced Auschwitz and Belsen.

Throughout the terrible years I had felt that I was being protected by an all-powerful being, but that source of assurance had begun to give way to some troubling questions. Why had I been spared and not millions of others, including my brother and father? Was the world improving as a result of its experience of mass annihilation? Was it not necessary to tell that story again and again and to look at it from every angle? How much time was left for the handful of survivors, before their unimaginable memories, which only they could bring to life, would be forgotten? Did not I and the other survivors owe a duty to the millions of victims to make it less likely that their deaths had been in vain?

I became convinced that if I could move only a handful of people to care more for their fellow man, I would achieve something worthwhile and that it was my duty to try to do just that.

I decided to approach my friend Evelyn Kent to help me write the story of my Holocaust experiences. I had not said more than a few words when she interrupted me and said: "Eva, I've been waiting ever since I first met you twenty years ago, to write your story."

That is how we came to write this book.

FAMILY TREE

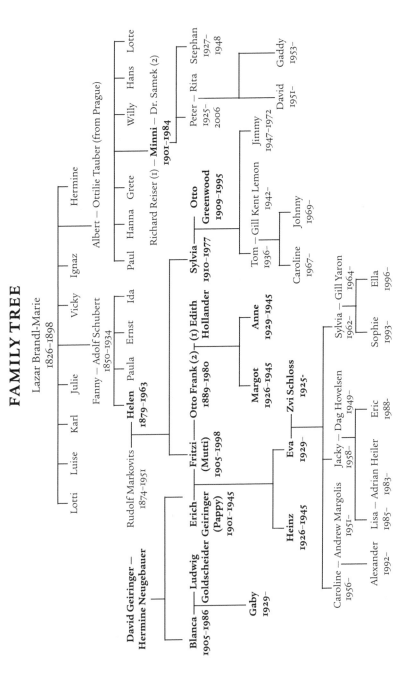

Part 1

FROM VIENNA TO AMSTERDAM

I

Refugees

For several years after the horror I had the recurring nightmare . . . *I am walking along a sunny street that suddenly becomes sinister. I am about to fall into a black hole* . . . I would wake up sweating and trembling. It haunted me on nights when I least expected it, but I got rid of it by repeating to myself, *"It's all over, thank God. I'm alive."*

So I got on with my daily life in England without talking much about the past because I have suppressed the memories for so long.

Now I want to acknowledge the miracle and remember clearly those who helped me to survive Birkenau. I owe them so much and don't want to forget them.

I WAS BORN in Vienna on 11 May 1929. My mother, Elfriede Markovits — Fritzi for short — came from an assimilated middle-class Jewish family. She was vivacious and beautiful, and at the age of eighteen she married twenty-one-year-old Erich Geiringer, an attractive and enterprising Austrian businessman.

It was love at first sight, they always told me. My mother was tall and fair, and my father had dark hair, piercing blue eyes and a flashing smile that women found hard to resist. Together they made a striking couple.

Fritzi and Erich — Mutti and Pappy to me — adored one another and, in the carefree days of their early marriage, they were part of a large circle of newlyweds who would meet at weekends to go hiking in the Austrian mountains. My father was full of energy, a fitness fanatic who enjoyed all outdoor activities and sports.

In 1926 they were blessed with a son whom they called Heinz Felix, and when I came along three years later, they were overjoyed to have a daughter to complete the family.

My mother's parents and her sister lived nearby, so Mutti took us to see them every day. My parents were not religious in the strictly Orthodox Jewish sense. They liked to feel they were an integral part of the Austrian community, but they had close Jewish friends whose children were my childhood friends. When I went to school, I began to understand what being Jewish meant, because all Jewish children were separated from the rest of the class during scripture. We had our own religious lessons in which we learnt prayers in Hebrew, some Jewish history and observances. Heinz and I appreciated our inheritance, and when we asked Mutti to light candles on Friday evening to welcome in the Sabbath, she did it to please us, but we were only taken to synagogue on High Holy days.

While Heinz and I were growing up, Pappy liked to encourage a feeling of resilience and self-reliance in us. "You must never be afraid," he would say, throwing me into the deep end of a swimming pool when I was very young while Mutti stood gasping with fright at the side.

When I was three, sometimes he would sit me on the top of our large wardrobe and tell me to jump down into his arms or remain up there. In spite of my fear, I trusted him and of course he always caught me. I enjoyed these challenges, but Heinz was much more sensitive and although he was three years older, he was often frightened by them.

During holidays Pappy would take us climbing in the Tirolean Mountains and the Austrian Alps. It was all an exciting adventure for me. Once, when I was four, we lost our way for many hours and my mountain boots became so uncomfortable that I took them off and happily climbed barefoot over the rocks.

Sometimes Pappy would tie a rope ladder to a tree or a rock at the top of a precipice, and he and I would climb down it like Tarzan while Mutti and Heinz waited for us to return. I worshipped Pappy and loved to copy him. Unlike Heinz, I shared his love of physical sports, and I was determined to be tough for his sake.

"It is bad for your posture to sleep on soft mattresses and pillows," Pappy said to us once. So, on our next Sunday outing, I brought home a large flat stone to use as a pillow. Heinz and I shared a bedroom, and to my annoyance he laughed at me.

I was a fussy eater, and although I was perfectly healthy, I was very skinny. Mutti would make me take a spoonful of cod liver oil daily, which made me sick. I would have loved plates of spaghetti and sausages, but instead I had to eat red cabbage and spinach, which I hated. Mutti would insist that I eat it all up. If I refused to eat much or to do as I was told, I would be made to stand in the corner. I had a defiant, rebellious streak in me, and I would refuse to apologize even when I knew I had been wrong.

Heinz was a different character, more obedient and with more creative talent than me.

"You are the practical one, Evi," Mutti would say fondly, "but Heinz is the clever one."

He read voraciously and had a vivid imagination. He would intrigue me with tales of his favorite author of Westerns, Karl May. He would pretend to be Winnetou, a Red Indian, while I would imagine I was his old partner, Shatterhand. Sometimes when we were alone together in our bedroom he would make up ghost stories and whisper them in low, mysterious tones that terrified and excited me at the same time. He would play the beam of his torch on to the ceiling: red, green, yellow — dancing in patterns that made me think there really was a ghost in the room.

Heinz found a way to make me cry simply by telling me a story in which he was an old man, alone, deserted and about to die with no one in the world to grieve for him. His voice would become cracked and aged, and I became so involved that I would sob my heart out. We made a pact to use this trick when there were visitors in our house. Heinz would say, "I bet I can make Eva cry in three minutes without touching her!"

Sure enough, as he began to recount the story, I would burst into tears. I could not bear to think of him dying.

When he was seven, Heinz developed an eye infection which was incorrectly diagnosed and, as a result, his condition became chronic. My parents were very worried about him. When he was nine, despite countless visits to specialists and hospitals, he eventually went blind in one eye. He accepted this stoically and did not allow it to spoil his childhood.

My brother and I were part of a happy and close-knit family, with grandparents, aunts, uncles and cousins who enjoyed each other's company. In those early years we had little suspicion that Jews in Vienna, whether religious or not, were about to come under an evil threat. Hitler and the Nazis had come to power in Germany in 1933, when I was four years old, bringing waves of anti-Semitic demonstrations.

In Germany attacks on Jews and their property were actively encouraged. On 12 March 1938, amid great rejoicing by the Austrians, the Germans marched into Austria and the atmosphere in Vienna changed overnight. Non-Jewish acquaintances suddenly became openly hostile to us. Many Jews now realized the danger they were in and hurriedly left for Holland, Britain or the USA.

Of the people in our family, Mutti's younger sister, Sylvi, together with her husband, Otto Grunwald (later Greenwood), and baby son, Tom, left for England in August 1938. They settled in Darwen, Lancashire, where there was much unemployment. As an expert in the Bakelite process (a forerunner of modern plastics), Otto had been given permission by the British government to go into business as a consultant to a manufacturer of umbrella handles. One year later he sent for Mutti's parents, who were able to join him just before the outbreak of war.

Pappy's sister, Blanca, had married an art historian, Ludwig Goldscheider. Their daughter, Gaby, was a month older than me and my best friend. They immediately fled to London. Phaedon Press, the art publishing house for which Uncle Ludwig worked, later transferred its business from Vienna to England and remained a successful publisher of art books.

My father, too, decided to make plans for emigration to a safer country. He thought of moving his shoe business to the south of Holland where this industry was concentrated. Thus we would have a choice of living either in Brussels or Amsterdam. Mutti wanted to reestablish the family in a cosmopolitan city which in many respects would be similar to Vienna and she favored Brussels, mainly because of the language. All of the family spoke good French except me, as I was too young to have been taught any languages except my native German.

Pappy had always manufactured shoes. He had inherited his first factory from his father, but that had failed in the economic depression of 1933. After that he had the idea of creating a cottage industry to make moccasins. He employed women in their homes to knit the multicolored tops which were sewn onto leather soles by a group of shoemakers from his old factory. This enterprise proved so successful that Pappy was soon exporting moccasins to the USA and Holland and aiming to build up a reserve of capital in a Dutch bank. In May 1938 he left us in Vienna while he took his manufacturing technique to Holland and went into partnership with the owner of a failing shoe factory. Soon his flair began to turn the losses into profits.

His determination to send for us as soon as possible was strengthened when Heinz returned from school one afternoon with blood streaming down his face from a cut eye. He had been bullied and thoroughly beaten up by the other boys in his class simply because he was a Jew. Mob rule was beginning to take over, and we had no defense against that.

After this attack my parents decided to send Heinz on alone to stay with Pappy in Brabant for the time being. Mutti was left behind with me to sell as many of our possessions as possible. She knew that we would not be allowed to take much money out of Austria, so she decided to equip me for the next two years. We went on a shopping trip around Bitman, a large children's store in the center of Vienna, where she spent a great deal of money buying me clothes, most of which I liked. She bustled into the coat department.

"We are going to live in Brussels," Mutti confided to the eager sales assistant, "and I want a very smart coat and hat for my daughter."

"I have the very thing," she said and, to my horror, she reappeared holding a bright orange woollen coat with a Scottish tartan hat to match the collar. I thought it was hideous.

"I am not going to wear that!" I exclaimed.

"Of course you will," said Mutti. "All the little Belgian girls are wearing smart coats like this."

She looked at the assistant, who nodded with approval. I hoped it wouldn't fit me.

"A fraction too large," said Mutti. "Very satisfactory, there's just enough room for you to grow into it."

In spite of my protests she bought the coat, but, I thought stubbornly, not even Mutti could make me wear it.

When we arrived home that evening, there was a letter from Pappy urging us to join him in Breda, Brabant. A week later, in June 1938, we left Austria for good to stay with Pappy and Heinz in a private house as paying guests.

Breda was a small provincial Dutch town in the southern part of Holland near the Belgian border. It was different in every way from the metropolitan life of Vienna, and to me it was like a holiday in the country. The last few weeks had been a great strain on us all. Just for the moment at least we were together again and away from the threatening atmosphere of Vienna. In contrast to the Austrians, the Dutch were homely, friendly people who made us feel very welcome.

Everyone in Holland seemed to own a bicycle, and one sunny Sunday, as a special treat, we hired four bicycles for a day out. We had a picnic in the warm, peaceful countryside, and as I lay on the grass gazing at clouds, I thought how lucky I was not to be going to school the next day. I knew that when I joined a school in Brussels the lessons would be in French, and I could not imagine how I was going to cope.

It was a short respite before the upheavals that were to

come. By the end of July arrangements had been made for me and Heinz to go to schools in Belgium. Mutti, Heinz and I moved to a boarding house on the outskirts of Brussels, and Pappy promised to visit us every weekend. Almost overnight we had become refugees.

The owner of the boarding house was Belgian, an M. LeBlanc, who had married a French widow with a son called Jacky. He was nine, the same age as me, and we struck up a friendship. He taught me that people can be friends without understanding each other's language. We played together, becoming good companions, and all the time I was picking up French without realizing it.

Our family slept in two rooms. I shared one with Heinz, and Mutti shared her tiny double bedroom with Pappy on weekends. We ate our meals in a large communal dining room with other families, German and Czechoslovakian Jews, in the same predicament as ourselves. An elderly French dowager sat in one corner and in the other a middle-aged bachelor retired from the civil service in the Belgian Congo. He was a sinister man who made me very frightened.

One day Jacky and I went into his room when he was out and saw a dangerous-looking collection of weapons, spears and lances, hanging on his wall. We were examining them with great curiosity when we heard him coming. As a joke, just to frighten him we jumped up and screamed. Without hesitation he tore a Congolese spear from the wall and lunged towards us. We rushed out of the room in panic and after that made sure we kept out of his way!

Some afternoons I accompanied Mutti to the center for refugees where people could make contact with one another, getting advice and assistance with all kinds of practical problems: where adults could go for French lessons; how to report to the police; how to get some financial help. There was end-less filling in of forms. It was a transit center for many on their way out to Britain and America, and one day my grand-parents even arrived to stay at our boarding house for a few days before they went on to England.

In the evenings we had nowhere to sit except in our bed-rooms. I would lie on my bed watching disconsolately as Heinz conscientiously studied his Latin and French home-work. He had no time for me, so I would eventually go down to the courtyard to play with Jacky. There was a case that was full of his mother's old clothes, and we would dress our-selves up and pretend to be grown-ups until Mutti called me to bed.

Even in "digs" Mutti tried to keep my life as normal as possible by sending me to the local school. How could it be normal for me? For eight years I'd heard and spoken only German, and suddenly all the lessons were in French. I was in despair. I couldn't understand even the simplest instruction. Other children tried to help me, but soon gave up when they realized I hadn't understood one word. The lessons were quite different from my old school where we had worked out sim-ple sums on paper. Here the children seemed to know it in their heads, so when the teacher called out what sounded like multiplication tables they would immediately shout out the answers. I could only sit there, dumb and miserable.

The pretty young teacher did her best to encourage me, but I was desperately unhappy. After a month she tried to in-volve me in the lessons. One day she dictated a short story in French, and all the children, including me, had to write it down in their exercise books with the correct spelling. Next day, when the work was handed back marked, everybody had to call out the number of their mistakes. My page was covered in red, my mistakes as many as the words in the story. I felt so humiliated that I ran home to Mutti in tears.

Mutti decided that I should learn twenty words every day: she would teach me the French words for familiar objects and make me repeat them after her. Then I would write them down and try to learn them. There were so many new words that by Friday I had forgotten what I'd learnt on Monday, which made Mutti so frustrated with me (on top of all her other worries) that she would slap me hard. So there were even more tears at the end of those lessons.

"You're such a stubborn child," Mutti would say in exasperation — which was quite true since by then I had refused to wear the orange coat and Mutti had had to dye it navy.

9 November 1938
Krystal Nacht, the burning of 7,500
Jewish shops and synagogues in Germany

Gradually the dense fog of a new language began to lift. Towards Christmas there was an Open Evening for the class. All parents, including Mutti and Pappy, came to sit at the side of the classroom while each of us had some poetry to recite. Our teacher introduced us as, one by one, we stood at the front of the class to say our piece. She had given me a fable of La Fontaine — it was quite long but I was determined to do my best to learn it by heart in fluent French. When it was my turn, she introduced me as "a little Austrian Jewish girl who has worked very hard." This was quite true, but as I walked nervously to the front, the poem went quite out of my head. I stood there, dumbly looking at the rows of faces.

"Come on, Eva, it's your turn now," she said.

I opened my mouth and to my astonishment all the

words came flooding out as if I'd known them all my life, and when I came to the end everyone applauded. As I looked at my parents and Heinz, who were smiling proudly, I felt really pleased with myself.

15 March 1939
Germany invades Bohemia and Moravia (Czechoslovakia)

After my Open Evening success I felt part of the class and began to enjoy school. I would skip back to Mutti after school to tell her my news, but for her life was far less simple and carefree. She missed being in charge of her own home, and she was more aware of the danger of our position as stateless refugees. She missed grandmother very much, with all her dominating advice on how to bring us up, and the companionship of Auntie Silvi and Auntie Blanca. Although there were one or two friends she had met at the center for refugees, there were no lighthearted get-togethers anymore. Pappy would try to commute from the factory in Brabant most weekends, but we all missed the security of our own home.

At the beginning of May, close to my ninth birthday, I longed to have a party and ask friends from school.

"Oh please, Mutti," I nagged. "I do so want a party and to blow out my candles on a cake!"

"Well, alright, Eva," she said reluctantly, "but we will have to ask Madame LeBlanc first."

To my delight she agreed.

"Only a small party of six, mind, in my dining room," she said. "But I will make a cake especially for you."

I was so happy! I eagerly wrote the invitations to hand out to my three special friends in class. At breaktime they asked me what presents I would like, and we excitedly decided together what games we would play. But the following morning all three told me that their parents would not allow them to come. I could not believe it. Why? I was bewildered and very hurt. I think that it was then that I began to realize what it meant to be Jewish at that time. It hit me hard and I felt like an outcast.

23 August 1939
Nazi-Soviet Non-Aggression Pact

In August Pappy took us to a small boarding house in Zandvoort, Holland, for a holiday by the sea. The weather was perfect. We spent two carefree weeks running along the dunes, swimming together in the sea and splashing each other with water. Everything seemed glorious. I was full of joy until we returned to Brussels and school at the end of the month.

1 September 1939
Germany invades Poland

3 September
Britain declares war on Germany

4 September
France declares war on Germany

At the beginning of September a lot happened very quickly. When war between England and Germany broke out, Pappy realized that borders between Holland and Belgium were likely to close, so he took immediate steps for us to live with him in Holland. As alien refugees, however, we had to wait until February 1940 for the appropriate papers to come through, and only then were we able to join him.

2

Amsterdam

We rented a furnished apartment on the first floor in a secluded, modern square in Amsterdam, Niew Zuid at 46 Merwedeplein. Although life was full of uncertainty and fear because of the war, I felt much more content and secure because we were together again as a family. That, for me, was the only thing that mattered.

I was growing fast. As soon as we arrived in Holland, Pappy stood Heinz and me up against our bedroom wall and drew pencil marks of our heights.

"Now you have made your marks here," he said, "so this room is yours."

When he measured me a month later, I was delighted to discover I had grown half an inch — and so had Heinz.

My brother and I shared the back bedroom, which led out on to a small balcony with an icebox in the corner. Once a week the ice man came round, and Heinz would have to carry up a huge block of ice wrapped in sacking to place at the bottom of the fridge where Mutti kept milk, butter, cheese and meat. Sometimes we would creep out in the middle of the night and help ourselves to a sausage for a midnight feast. We would sit on our beds munching and whispering and having fun. After the formality of the boarding house it was wonderful to have our own home.

Residents in the square had to take part in fire and air-raid drills, so Mutti and Pappy soon made friends with other Jewish families. There was a spirit of comradeship between them, with neighbors helping to keep each other cheerful. Pappy made good friends with a neighbor, Martin Rosenbaum. He was a kind man, married to an Austrian Christian, Rosi. They had no children, but he often complimented Pappy about us.

"What delightful children you have, Erich," he would say, "and so talented."

This was certainly true of Heinz. Mutti had been delighted to find a baby grand piano in the lounge of the apartment. Both she and Heinz played well, and Heinz was soon taking piano lessons again. He would practice Chopin exercises followed by jazz music which he could play by ear. *"Bei mir bist du sheyn,* again and again, *bei mir bist du sheyn* means you're grand." I loved dancing round the room while he played, pretending I was on the stage while Mutti or Pappy applauded me.

Mutti found a cellist and violinist among her new acquaintances. They came up to the apartment once a week to practice chamber music. It was too much for Pappy. As the squeaky violin started, he would say he was "just going out to get some fresh air" and nip over to Martin's apartment to escape. I would see them strolling away together.

Once again I was sent to the local primary school, and I resigned myself to having to learn yet another tongue. It was Dutch but easier this time because the Flemish I had heard in Belgium once a week was similar. At least I could understand a little: most Dutch primary schools taught French and by now my French was almost fluent.

This had its drawbacks because I thought I was better than the teacher. Whenever she mispronounced a French word — which was often — I corrected her. It made me feel very important, but she was furious and took it out on me during the rest of the lessons. She was really nasty to me, but I didn't care because it made me a great success with the rest of the class.

The daily routine at home gave me the security I had not experienced for a long time. In the early spring evenings I could hear the sounds of children playing outside in the square below. It seemed a perfect place for games — a no-through road in the shape of a triangle with a grassy space at one end edged with newly planted bushes and trees. All the youngsters from the surrounding flats and streets gathered there to size each other up and play together.

Many Jewish families had been living in that area since 1933, so by this time the Jewish children were in tight cliques which tended to keep newcomers out. I would stand around waiting for someone to talk to me, anxious to join in, but they did not want me. I was glad when some of my Dutch schoolfriends came into the square and asked me to be their friend. I suppose I was a novelty, but before long I was playing marbles with them, marking out patches for hopscotch or playing skipping games. Then Pappy bought me a black second-hand bicycle to ride and do tricks on like everybody else. In the early months of 1940, as I rode around with my friends wearing the required uniform of navy raincoat and Wellington boots, I felt at last that I really belonged. Often, when it wasn't raining, there were enough children to make up teams for games like rounders. That was the best part because it required the process of picking sides, and as I was a good batter and runner everyone suddenly wanted to pick me, which restored my self-esteem.

GRADUALLY I BEGAN to recover my natural high spirits. Life seemed to be improving all round. Birds sang in the lengthening April evenings and, after reporting home from school, I would dash out into the square to join in the games and become one of the gang. At six my mother would call me in for supper, but I was always reluctant to leave and would protest loudly — after all, some children were still outside after eight! — but Pappy insisted that I was not to be out later than supper time. Unlike Mutti, I was not gentle and docile: I had inherited Pappy's strong character and he enforced many "house arrests" on me for stubbornness. I was so brimful of verve and energy that I always wanted to be outside in the thick of things.

In time I began to make special friends. I developed a crush on Suzanne Lederman. She had luminous violet eyes, peach skin and thick dark plaits that reached halfway down her back. I hung around her all the time, but she wanted to be with two lively girls called Anne and Hanne. This selective group of three went around together. We nicknamed them Anne, Hanne and Sanne because they were an inseparable trio, each of them a little more sophisticated than the rest of us — more like teenagers. They did not want to join in with our childish games and would sit together watching us and giggling over the boys, which I thought was silly. They were always looking at fashion magazines and collecting pictures of film stars.

I could look across to Suzanne's bedroom window from my room, and sometimes we would send messages to one another. One warm Sunday afternoon when I was sitting with Suzanne on the steps of our apartment, she confided in me how much she admired her friend Anne Frank because she was so stylish.

It was quite true. Once, when Mutti had taken me to the local dressmaker to have a coat altered, we were sitting waiting our turn and heard the dressmaker talking to her customer inside the fitting room. The customer was very determined to have things just right.

"It would look better with larger shoulder pads," we could hear her saying in an authoritative tone of voice, "and the hemline should be just a little higher, don't you think?"

We then heard the dressmaker agreeing with her, and I sat there wishing I was allowed to choose exactly what I wanted to wear. I was flabbergasted when the curtains were drawn back and there was Anne, all alone, making decisions about her own dress. It was peach-colored with a green trim.

She smiled at me. "Do you like it?" she said, twirling around.

"Oh, yes!" I said breathlessly in great envy. I was not up to that standard! Anne appeared so much more grown-up than me, even though I was a month older. She attended the local Montessori school and was a whole year ahead of me in her school work.

Anne's apartment was opposite ours in the same square. I often went over there because I wanted to be near Suzanne. The Franks also had a large tabby cat that purred appreciatively when I picked it up. I longed to fondle a pet of my own, but Mutti firmly refused to allow me one. I would wander into the sitting room to cuddle the cat and find Mr. Frank watching me with amused eyes. He was much older than Pappy and very kind. When he realized how little Dutch I knew, he always made a point of talking to me in German. Mrs. Frank would prepare lemonade for the children, and we would sit drinking together in the kitchen.

Heinz had developed a crush on two girls, both of whom

lived in the same square as us. One, Ellen, was a Jewish immigrant like ourselves but the other, Jopie, was a pretty Dutch blonde. I resented the attention he paid them — in fact, I did not like the idea of my brother paying attention to any other girl. I became quite jealous. After all, I was his little sister and I was intensely proud of him, of his musical gifts and brilliant mind. Apart from this, nothing much else troubled me. Spring was here and I loved Amsterdam, where my life was at last returning to normal.

10 May 1940
German invasion of Holland and Belgium

We had thought that we were safe living in Holland and were settling down to enjoying our new life when, to everyone's shock, the Nazis invaded Holland.

On 13 May my family with thousands of others went down to the port trying to get on a ship to escape to England. We queued for hours but in vain. All the ships had either left or were full, and we were eventually turned back and told we were too late.

14 May 1940
German Luftwaffe bombs Rotterdam to force capitulation of Holland. After five days Holland surrenders.

The country was now under the total control of the Nazis. German soldiers were everywhere. Although the Germans announced at first that nothing was going to change, each week new regulations to restrict us were announced over the radio and on posters.

Hitler decreed that Jewish children had to go to Jewish

schools that were to be opened specially for them. They were not to be allowed to mix with other children in Dutch schools, and Jewish teachers had to be found as Christians were not allowed to teach us.

Until that time Heinz had attended the lyceum (secondary school). He now had to go to the Jewish School, where he met Margot Frank, Anne's elder sister, and they became quite friendly, often doing their homework together. They had a lot in common — both were academically gifted and ambitious to do well in their studies. My parents managed to find a private tutor for me and I attended his home with some other children to continue my school work.

All Jews now had to be inside their homes before eight every evening and were not allowed to attend cinemas, concerts or theaters. We were not allowed to use the trams or trains. We could only do our shopping between the hours of three and five in the afternoon, and we could only use Jewish shops. All Jews had to wear a bright yellow Star of David (Magen David) on their clothes so that they were instantly recognizable.

On 19 February 1941 400 young Jews from Amsterdam Zuid aged between twenty and thirty-five were rounded up. On 25 February, the Dutch trade unions organized a General Strike in sympathy, and all transport and services in Amsterdam came to a halt for two days. The Germans threatened to take hostages and kill them if normal life did not resume immediately. Even then some brave Dutch Christians started to wear the yellow star in sympathy with us and to confuse the Germans.

Mutti had to buy the stars for our clothes. Every outside piece of clothing had to show a yellow star.

"Never take off your coat if your dress has not got a star on it," Mutti warned me as I watched her sew them onto my navy coat and jumper. "If any Jew is stopped and is not show-ing the star, the Germans will arrest them."

As time went by, during 1941 and 1942, we began to feel in-creasingly frightened. Pappy was at home with us now be-cause he had been prevented from traveling to the factory in Brabant. He came up with the idea of manufacturing small round snake-leather handbags from cast-off snake-skins and soon the business became a flourishing cottage industry giv-ing work to others who had lost their jobs because of the Nazi decrees. It gave him the means to support us and save for a time when he himself might not be able to work.

He went out to many meetings to discuss the worsening situation with other Jews. One evening he sat us down to-gether and warned us that we might have to go into hiding. He felt we would have a better chance if we separated and went into two hiding places. When I started to cry at the thought, he explained that continuing the family line was im-portant to him, that people achieved a kind of immortality through the memories of their children and grandchildren, and that we would double our chances of survival by splitting up. Meanwhile he was going to acquire false identity papers for the time when we would be forced to conceal our Jewish identity.

The Dutch had organized themselves to form under-ground resistance groups to fight the hated Germans. Pappy made contact with them, and they provided him with false papers which identified us as true Dutch citizens, not Jewish, with quite different names and background.

Mutti was to be Mefrouw Bep Ackerman, but although I remembered my new name, which was Jopie Ackerman, I kept forgetting my false date of birth and where I had been born, so Mutti had to keep coaching me.

Naturally Heinz knew his part by heart. By this time he was fifteen, tall, and rather Jewish-looking, which worried him. I did not need to worry because I was born with bright blue eyes, fair skin and fair hair, so that I looked exactly like any other little Dutch girl. Mutti had the tall, elegant stance of a Scandinavian, and her looks would not give her away either. She sold some of her jewelry to have some ready cash on hand.

Another concern was our health. Mutti and Pappy knew that if we went into hiding, it would be very difficult to get medical assistance if we became ill. For several weeks I had been suffering from severe tonsillitis, and it was decided that I would need to have my tonsils taken out.

By that time it was too dangerous for a Jew to go into hospital, as many who were admitted were arrested and transported directly from the wards. A local doctor agreed to operate on me in his surgery where I was strapped into a chair and given laughing gas. The gas had a strange effect on me. As I began to regain consciousness, I dreamt that the whole room was on fire and everything around me was burning. I woke up in terror. My parents carried me home and I lay in bed for a week, unable to speak and only able to eat ice-cream. Mutti and Heinz were very attentive, and Pappy told me how brave I had been. But when my throat healed and I was able to eat properly again, I began to develop fast and I grew up, both mentally and physically.

None of the children in the square talked about their family secrets. We trusted our parents to cope with whatever situation might arise. In any case, I did not want to think about the future too much because I was happy as I was. I could not face the thought that it might mean separation from Heinz. I adored him and wanted to stay with him. In fact, I wanted everything to go on being the same, but Mutti and Pappy knew this was not possible and had planned carefully for what they felt would be the inevitable outcome of the Nazi persecution of the Jews.

I can recall walks along sunny streets that were beginning to feel threatening. I remember Heinz returning from school one afternoon very agitated. His friend Walter had taken off his jacket because it was a warm day, and since he was no longer showing the yellow star, SS men had stopped them and arrested Walter. I felt that an immense evil was about to engulf us.

1942
Germans push towards Stalingrad

Pappy rented an empty room in a storehouse on the Singel alongside the canal, where he put trunks to be filled with provisions for our hiding. By now food was already rationed, so we had to make every effort to save from our weekly allocation.

I remember I had a brown paper parcel to carry. Heinz had pushed it into my satchel, helping me to loop the strap over my head so that the bag sat on my right hip. It was heavy for me, containing six tins of condensed milk and six tins of sardines, a packet of rice and a tin of cocoa. I watched Heinz fill his school case with tins of tomato puree, a bottle of olive oil, sugar and some chocolate bars. Mutti and Pappy were also preparing parcels of food to put into their bags.

By now it was springtime, April 1942, when yellow and pale green buds tipped the branches of the willow and plane trees alongside the canals. Mutti and Pappy walked together in front, Pappy with his attaché case and Mutti carrying her basket; Heinz and I walked behind them along cobbled streets beside the canal, over little bridges and down towards the warehouses. My satchel was heavy and my shoelace came undone. As I leaned against a stone wall to tie up my lace, the tins clanked and I suddenly felt terribly afraid. But Heinz was there to put his hand under my satchel to steady it for me. I loved him for it. It was Sunday with fewer people about, but there was a market further along the lanes, so we pretended we were going there.

As soon as we arrived at the wooden door to the warehouse, we entered quickly and climbed up two flights of stairs to our storeroom. Pappy unlocked the door, and we went inside to unload our packages and tins.

"Put the tomatoes in this suitcase with the olive oil and rice," he instructed us efficiently, "and the sardines and chocolate over here."

"Shall I put the condensed milk with the cocoa?" I said. These were important issues to me, and I wanted to help in any way I could.

After we had packed the goods away, we covered them with clothing and sprinkled mothballs on top. We were to return there many times. As it turned out, our secret hoard did provide the nourishment to help people survive the terrible privations of the war — but not us.

ON THE MORNING of 6 July a card arrived by post for Heinz. It gave instructions for him to report with a rucksack in three days' time to the old theatre nearby. From there he was to be sent to a labor camp somewhere in Germany. Mutti was desperate, but Heinz tried to comfort her.

"I'll go, Mutti," he said bravely. "After all, my friends will be there too. Henk, Marcel and Margot had their cards too, so we will all be together."

"It will be slave labor," sobbed Mutti.

"They won't harm me if I work hard," Heinz said, looking to Pappy for agreement.

"Young people will be useful to them," muttered Pappy, "but I think it is time we disappeared."

Within twenty-four hours all the appropriate arrangements had been finalized. Pappy and Heinz were to make their way to a separate hiding place. It had all been organized by the Dutch underground. Mutti and I were going to an address of a teacher, a Mrs. Klompe, on the other side of Amsterdam Zuid.

We spent the last few hours together as a family. When it was time to part, I clung on to my tall, handsome father.

"Pappy, I don't want to go without you," I cried. I could not bear the thought of being parted from him again.

"Evertje, be a grown-up girl now," he said. "You must look after Mutti for me."

My arms were around his neck, and my toes were off the ground as he hugged me. And then, when he set me on my feet again, he held my shoulders and looked at me very seriously and whispered as if in prayer, *"God bless and keep you."* Suddenly I felt a great strength flow into me, and I stopped protesting and stood quietly.

Heinz stood beside me with tears running down his face. He brushed them away with his hand, put his arms around me and kissed me good-bye.

I remember walking away from the apartment with Mutti. This time we wore jackets without yellow stars, and I held a magazine self-consciously over my chest to hide the fact that I was not wearing it. I looked around the square where the children used to gather. In the early morning light everything seemed deserted and forlorn. We had not been able to say good-bye to anyone and I was worried that I would be missed by my friends that afternoon because they would not know what had happened to me. Our friendly milkman was standing outside with his milk-float, but he turned his head away, pretending not to have seen us as we hurried out into the square.

Holding a small bag each, Mutti and I walked silently across Amsterdam to Mrs. Klompe's house. We knocked on the door, which was opened by a well-groomed, middle-aged lady. We had never met her before, but she said quite loudly for the benefit of any nosey neighbors, "How are you? It's wonderful to see you again," and she stood smiling at us repeating, "Come in! Come in!"

She was trying not to look conspiratorial, but as we crossed the threshold, she closed the door quickly behind us and led us into her front room. Over a cup of tea she discussed arrangements with Mutti, then signalled us to follow her up three flights of stairs to the attic, which had been partitioned off into two rooms. One was a small bedroom where I was going to sleep. The other was a living room with a cupboard, table and three chairs. There was also a floral-patterned sofa where Mutti would sleep.

Down a few steps was a long room that was a bathroom with a toilet at the far end. We had no cooking facilities, but we were to use her kitchen downstairs and Mutti had agreed to cook her dinner as well.

"You cannot use either the bathroom or kitchen while I am out," she warned. "If the neighbors hear any noise, they will become suspicious. You will have to take great care to keep your presence here secret."

"How safe are we?" Mutti wondered aloud.

"The Germans make frequent raids to search out hidden

Jews," Mrs. Klompe said. "They are like ratcatchers intent on exterminating vermin," she continued drily, "but we in the underground are equally intent on protecting the innocent."

She smiled at me reassuringly, but I began to feel the sickening contraction of fear in my stomach.

That same evening our underground contact, a Mr. Broeksma, visited us. He was a teaching colleague of Mrs. Klompe, and they worked closely together. Being a Frieslander — one of the hardy outdoor people who took part in skating races in the midwinter along miles of frozen canal water — he was a fine and true Dutchman with fire in his belly against the invaders. He was intelligent, tough and reliable and, like the other underground workers, extremely resourceful. We were in his hands and he knew our peril, but we trusted him completely.

He took some time to survey our hiding place and then advised us that we would still need to have another secret place within its walls where we could conceal ourselves if searches were made on our block.

Of course, he had to organize everything. He found a builder and brought him the following evening when they both went over our tiny living space to determine how we might best be hidden. They finally decided that it would be safest to partition off the toilet from the rest of the bathroom.

They agreed to make a tiled wall which would have a kind of trapdoor in it so that it could be fitted back from the toilet side. From the outside it would simply look like a solid tiled wall. That meant we would have to climb through a hole every time we needed to use the toilet, but we could hide in there in cases of emergency.

All the materials had to be found, then brought to the

house during darkness, piece by little piece, but the two men managed to start work within a fortnight.

On the third Sunday of our hiding they worked all day until it was nearly finished. Only the trapdoor needed to be tiled. They were both, tired but they decided to stay late into the evening to complete the job. When they asked Mutti to try it out, she climbed in, sat herself on the toilet and lifted the heavy tiled trapdoor into place, disappearing behind a seemingly solid wall.

The two men looked at one another in approval and shook hands. When Mutti reemerged, they then shook hands with us and went away satisfied.

I was sound asleep by midnight, so the noises of vans in the street below and the heavy knocking at the front door only slowly penetrated through my dreams to bring me back to reality. Germans were downstairs shouting, "Are there any filthy Jews hiding here?"

"Mutti?" I was terrified as I felt Mutti grab hold of me.

"Quick, Eva, cover the bed with the counterpane," she whispered as she pulled me out of bed and helped me smooth down the covers as quickly as we could so that the bed did not look as if it had been slept in.

We ran into the bathroom and pushed ourselves into the tiny toilet compartment. We lifted the heavy trapdoor back into position and waited in the pitch dark. I could feel Mutti sitting on the toilet grasping her knees while I squatted down next to her.

We heard the sound of soldiers' boots stamping up the narrow stairs next to our wooden partition. I crouched in terror, my heart beating so loudly that I was sure they could hear it.

Suddenly the bathroom door was thrown open, and Germans were tramping into the room shouting to each other. There was a pause, and then we could hear them stamping noisily all over the house. Finally they gave up, and we heard them close the front door with a slam.

Mutti pulled my head against her face. I could feel that she was crying with relief. If they had raided the house two hours earlier, they would have found us. God in heaven and our Frieslanders had watched over us.

3

In Hiding

From the time Mutti and I went into hiding, I entered a seemingly protected world. My days were spent entirely in the company of my mother, and I remember them as full of warmth and love. During the next two years, hidden in our attic, she taught me German, French, geography and history out of books brought in by Mrs. Klompe. Once or twice a week Mr. Broeksma came to teach me Dutch and maths. I wanted to learn and occupied my time well, but, unlike Heinz, I was not extremely bright and it did not come easily to me. I struggled along on my own, missing the company of other pupils intensely. Sometimes I would lie on my bed yearning for the old times in the square when we raced around like mad things on our bicycles. In my tiny attic cubicle I would kick my legs high into the air and fling my body around in an agony of pent-up energy and frustration at being young and imprisoned.

But occasionally, very occasionally, there were days of joyful reunion with Pappy and Heinz. Their hiding place was in the countryside at Soesdijk, and it was truly perilous when we visited them because we had to travel by train. Oddly enough, we would never have dared to go out to the local shops for fear of being recognized by locals, but we did venture farther out by pretending that we were ending our visit to Mrs. Klompe.

Pappy's landlady, Mrs. De Bruin, allowed us to stay for the weekend, and we would return to Amsterdam on Monday morning with the commuters. On the rare glorious Fridays of our visit we would leave the house carrying our small suitcases and walk to the railway station. It was a strange sensation being outside again. But since we were both fair-skinned and looked like any other Dutch mother and daughter, with luck we could walk incognito in the crowd. Nevertheless, it was extremely risky: we were scared all the time, especially as we were occasionally stopped by police or soldiers at the station barrier when Mutti had to show her false identity card. As I was still under sixteen, I was not required to have one but I did have to have my story down pat if I was asked questions. I never was; I must have looked too authentic to arouse suspicion.

Invariably the trains were full of soldiers, and the SS often made searches during the journey. We tried to look unconcerned while having to rub shoulders with our bitterest enemies. This journey was always harrowing, but it was worth it all just to be with Pappy and Heinz.

As soon as we were united in Mrs. De Bruin's attic rooms, my parents would shut themselves away to be alone, and Heinz and I would be left to ourselves to talk. Overnight, Mutti shared Pappy's room, and I lay on a mattress on the floor in Heinz's room. In the darkness I would creep over to his bed and climb in next to him for a cuddle. We started kissing and hugging with the joy of being together again, until all our suppressed energy and budding sexuality began to arouse us. The kissing and cuddling became more and more furtively pleasant. We would start to pet each other, feeling blissful surges of adolescent love. We did not really do anything wrong, and we were very scared that our parents would find out what we were up to, but we could not help ourselves. We only had each other to love. When I was alone in my attic bed, I cried for Heinz, missing him more than anything.

Being in hiding was an immense strain on Pappy. Always a keen, active businessman with his work taking up a good deal of his time, he too had to find other ways to channel his energies. At first he started to paint in oils — landscapes and pictures of places he knew. Each time Mutti visited him she had to sit for her portrait. Then, more surprisingly, he began to write poetry which revealed a creative and sensitive nature we had not appreciated before. He would smile rather shyly and read out his compositions to us. We were, after all, his only audience, but Mutti was astonished at this other side of his personality. It explained the origins of many of Heinz's gifts.

Heinz had so many talents. He was an artist who painted with a flair for color. One of his paintings was of a little child playing on the floor with a train; another of an empty attic room with rays of light streaming on to a box of toys in the corner. But the most powerful picture was one of himself in despair. He sits at a table in the foreground with his head on his arms, while in the background lies a dying figure.

He was also a gifted musician able to compose serious music. He wrote poetry that was full of meaning. Added to this, he was an adept scholar. During the time of his hiding Heinz studied Italian without help, and on one of our visits he asked for Italian novels to read. He was thirsty for knowledge and determined not to waste any time of his "captivity" in idleness.

23 October 1942
El Alamein, Rommel defeated in North Africa

Every evening at nine Pappy would tune into the BBC news which went out in Dutch. I remember the thrill of excitement hearing the Victory theme from Beethoven's Fifth before the broadcasts. We heard the news of Rommel's defeat on one of our first visits to Pappy and hugged each other in elation. The war would soon be over.

Our parents taught us bridge, and often the four of us passed our evenings playing together. The calls confused me, but I became quite good at trumping. Pappy always made me feel so proud when I played with him, but Heinz and I were the best partners of all, especially when we beat Mutti and Pappy! We played quietly, whispering our calls because we were always aware that we might be heard. Everything had to be done in secret and as silently as possible. By this time Heinz had even been obliged to disguise his Jewish looks by bleaching his hair with peroxide — so that it was now a gingery blond color.

Things were made worse for Pappy because Mrs. De Bruin's neighbors were Dutch Nazis. She warned Pappy about them, assuring him that although she was on very friendly terms with them, it was only to avoid suspicion. However, this complicated the set-up because one day the Nazis asked if they could sleep in her house while they were having their bedroom redecorated. How could she refuse them?

She came upstairs in high terror and insisted that both men stay on their beds for the whole of the visit. She gave them a large supply of bread and milk, put a chamber pot next to them and forbade them to make one sound. In the end, the visit lasted for only two days, but the whole incident began to unnerve Pappy. It brought home the stark reality of being totally dependent upon the goodwill and courage of Mrs. De Bruin.

2 February 1943
Stalingrad: German Sixth Army surrenders

Till now it had seemed that the Germans were succeeding in Russia, but the turning point came when the Russians and their winter defeated the Germans. With Pappy we listened to the glorious news over the BBC that 91,000 Germans had been captured. Pappy felt the end was at last in sight.

However, the defeats in Africa and Russia only served to make the Germans more dedicated in their pursuit of the Jews. Rewards were offered for betraying Jews to the Gestapo, and Pappy realized that the novelty of hiding us was wearing thin and that he and Heinz were in great danger. His fears increased when Mrs. De Bruin became hostile, gradually giving them less food and making rude remarks. She demanded more and more money for hiding them, and the money was beginning to run out. This unpleasant situation dragged on for nearly eighteen months, by which time Pappy was extremely depressed. He kept begging Mutti to find them another hiding place.

Mutti and I were also in a predicament. When we arrived back in Amsterdam after one of our weekends away, we were met inside the door by Mrs. Klompe in a state of fright. The Gestapo had raided her house once again and threatened her.

"Sheltering you both is becoming too much of a strain," she said. She looked apologetic but was quite determined that we should go.

Of course we understood, but we had to wait for the help

of the underground before we could be resettled, by which time the relationship between us had become very tense.

Eventually we were taken to stay with people whom we had actually known before.

He was Mr. Reitsma, another brave Frieslander, married to a very talented Jewish artist. They were both elderly, and their son Floris lived with them. They were very kind and made us feel welcome for the short time that we were to be with them. Mrs. Reitsma was busy with her art commissions and was pleased to have Mutti take over the cooking from her.

By now food was extremely scarce in Holland, so Mutti decided to risk a visit to our secret storage room to fetch some of our hidden food. It was unnecessary for both of us to expose ourselves to the danger of being captured, so she went on her own and I waited in trepidation for her to return. Eventually, she brought back tins and packets of flour, rice, sugar, chocolates and cocoa, and we thought what a feast we were going to have. But although the food was in good condition, everything had the strangest taste of mothballs. At any rate, it was greatly appreciated, and we managed to take some extra food over to Pappy and Heinz on our next visit.

By this time Pappy was even more depressed and was again begging Mutti to try to find another hiding place for them. Mutti realized his life was becoming unbearable because when she arrived, Mrs. De Bruin had cornered her and remarked pointedly, "Your fur coat is smart. It's quite wasted on you since you only go out once or twice a month. I have to do all the shopping for your husband and son, so I suggest you give it to me."

It was more of a demand than a request, and Mutti felt she had to hand it over. We were being caught up in blackmail. We knew that moving Pappy and Heinz would not be easy, but when we returned to Amsterdam, we reported the situation to Mr. Broeksma. He did not seem very surprised.

"There is not much I can do," he said. "Theirs is not a unique situation. Many others are being blackmailed. Even more are being handed over to the Gestapo for cash."

Mutti turned white when she heard this, but she was determined to try to alleviate Pappy's suffering. On her own initiative she went to see a Christian friend, Doortje, to ask her advice. As it happened, there was a nurse in the flat below who was known to work for the underground. Doortje promised to contact her, and she soon had good news for us. They had found a hiding place in Amsterdam. It would be nearer to us, and we felt it would be safer all round.

It was certain that Mrs. De Bruin would not relinquish her source of income easily, so Pappy and Heinz made plans to escape during the night. They crept out of the house without detection and caught an early train into the city, where they were met by the nurse. She hurried them to their new place of refuge nearer to us.

Everything seemed to be going according to plan. When we visited Pappy and Heinz the next day, we all felt more content. Their new hiding place was in a huge, old house with enormous rooms, and the couple who owned it were particularly friendly and kind. There seemed to be less pressure on us now, and Mutti and I returned to our base at the Reitsmas that evening greatly reassured.

4

Capture

It was my fifteenth birthday, and this year it fell on a Tuesday. I woke early, snug in my little bedroom in the Reitsmas' house. I could hear the birds chirping, the sun was streaming through the window and I lay for a long time with my hands behind my head watching the trees outside the window and feeling good to be alive. The knowledge that Pappy and Heinz were safe nearby in their new quarters added to my happiness. We had visited them on Sunday, and I was hoping, as it was a special day, that I would be able to see them today too.

At half past eight in the morning the Reitsmas sat down with us in their dining room to have a celebration birthday breakfast. Mrs. Reitsma had placed a vase of hyacinths and tulips in the center of the table, and Floris, their twenty-year-old son, solemnly handed me a small parcel as I sat down. "Keep this as a surprise." he said. "Open it after breakfast."

How charming he is to me, I thought, blushing. I set the package carefully before me on the table. The wrapping paper had delicate pink roses painted on one side by the talented

Mrs. Reitsma. I was enchanted by it. I could hardly wait to open it, and the anticipation added to my excitement.

A sudden ring on the doorbell startled us. We were not expecting anyone. Who was calling at that time in the morning? Mr. Reitsma got up from the table and went downstairs to open the door. To our sickening horror we heard the Gestapo storming in. Floris immediately sprang up, jumped over the table straight out of the window and disappeared over the rooftops. Within seconds the Gestapo officers had run up the stairs into the room and now stood there, eyeing the rest of us. Petrified with fear, we gazed at them and at the guards behind them who were pointing guns into the room.

"*Verfluchte Juden!* It's them!" they shouted.

We were numb with shock. Without giving us time to take anything with us, they pushed us roughly downstairs and outside into the street to be marched to the Gestapo Headquarters a few streets away.

As the four of us were marched along, Mutti, who was desperate to save me, grabbed at the arm of the Dutch Nazi beside her and tried to convince him that I was not wholly Jewish. He pushed her to one side, but she kept blurting out anything she could think of to get me released.

"My daughter is not Jewish," she said. "I had an affair with a non-Jew — my dentist . . . she is really his . . . she is not really Jewish at all."

But it was no use. The faces of our captors were hardset and implacable. They had got what they had come for and had triumphed at last.

When we arrived at the red-brick secondary-school building that was now the Gestapo Headquarters, we were pushed into a detention room where there were already some other people who had been caught in this roundup.

Armed guards stood at the door, the windows were shut, and wooden chairs had been placed around the walls where forlorn captives sat staring at the ground or out into space. Our hearts sank in misery as we joined them. No one looked up or tried to communicate with us. I was much too tense to cry. I sat in a corner next to Mutti who whispered to me, "How?" We simply could not grasp how it had happened. We had not expected it at all — we had felt fairly secure. Despite the Nazi hatred of the Jews, we had trusted in the expertise of the Dutch underground. We sat for hours and waited.

One by one people were called out and taken away. Some were returned to the room to go on waiting, others were not. Nobody said a word. Occasionally one or two women cried quietly, but no one comforted them or asked those who returned what had happened . . . we did not dare.

Sometimes we could hear screams coming from the room next door. We heard the sounds of beatings, of people weeping and crying out in pain and of German voices raised in anger. We sat frozen to our chairs sickened by the noises of terror.

Eventually it was Mutti's turn. She squeezed my arm before they led her away. I strained to hear any sounds I could from the room next door, listening for her cries, but I heard nothing. I sat alone for about half an hour.

Then they came for me.

A POLICEMAN in green uniform *(Grune Polizei)* took me into a sparsely furnished room that had a picture of Hitler hanging on the wall. I was made to stand in front of two Gestapo officers seated at a large desk. They both looked at me intently for several seconds until one of them spoke to me in polite German.

"Tell us everything we want to know and you will see your mother," he said.

"You will be able to see your father and brother as well," said the other.

I gasped. I had not realized Heinz and Pappy had also been caught.

"My father and brother?" I blurted out, and then I was angry with myself for talking. Tears burnt behind my eyes, but I was not going to let them see me react again if I could help it. I was determined not to tell them anything.

"Of course, we have them as well," the officer smiled coldly at me.

I suddenly began to tremble violently. I could not stop myself as they started to interrogate me in German, one after the other firing questions at me in quick succession. I was absolutely terrified of them.

"How long have you been with the Reitsmas?"

"We were just visiting," I said.

"Where have you been hiding?" They pushed papers around to each other on the desk.

"I don't know," I lied. "We arrived in the dark. It was a house in Amsterdam, but I don't know where."

"Where did you get your ration card from?"

"Where did your mother get her money from?"

"Who helped you find places to hide?"

I pretended not to know anything. Somehow I managed to flannel my way through without giving anything away. I admitted I had lived in Merwedeplein, but they knew we had gone into hiding. I described our landlady as being someone as unlike Mrs. Klompe as I possibly could. I said she was short, dumpy and elderly and that I did not know her name.

After a while they gave up trying to get any more out of

me and sent me back to the waiting room. Mutti was not there, but I sat down feeling quite proud of myself. I was thinking what a good performance I had given when from the interrogation room came voices that I recognized, first of Pappy and then Heinz. Their voices were raised in shouts which soon turned to screams followed by an awful silence.

My immediate reaction was that I was imagining it; that I was not really hearing it. I could not believe that it was happening. I thought the Gestapo were somehow bluffing to make me more afraid and give myself away. I listened intently, but I heard no other sounds. I began to feel sick with fear.

After a period of silence they called me in again. Once more I stood alone before the Gestapo. This time the senior officer looked at me scathingly and said, "We intend to torture your brother to death unless you cooperate with us."

I was horrified. I stared at them dumbly, not knowing what I was supposed to say.

"We will show you what we will do to him," he continued and nodded to someone behind me.

I was rooted to the spot in terror as the first truncheon blow landed across my shoulders. I suddenly realized that this was all really happening to me, that it was not a nightmare, that it was all true. The impact of the blows shot through me as they struck across my back and shoulders. They were quite relentless. I tried to fend them off with my arms, but I could not get out of their way. I knew they wanted me to scream so that they could threaten my father and make him talk. I tried so hard not to, but eventually I began to cry out. I could hear screams coming from inside me that I could not control.

As soon as they felt they had got enough noise out of me, they stopped. I was pushed roughly into another room with other men and women who had been similarly treated. Some had bruises on their faces; one or two had blood on their clothes. All were distressed and subdued.

Throughout that whole day, my fifteenth birthday, I was kept prisoner in a room without food or water, having to listen through the walls to people being interrogated, bullied and beaten. It lasted until evening.

At long last I was taken out and marched down a corridor to another room. As the door opened, I saw my parents standing there together looking towards me. Heinz was with them and the Reitsmas too. No one else was in the room. We fell into each other's arms, all crying and sobbing together as the door closed behind us and we were left to ourselves. Pappy told us that when we had visited him and Heinz on the Sunday afternoon in their new refuge, the nurse and their seemingly kind hosts had been informers working on both sides. They must have arranged to have us followed to discover where we were hiding and, having betrayed us, had probably received a substantial financial reward.

When we had calmed down a little, Pappy said, "Mutti has made a deal with the Gestapo. She is going to give them our box of talcum powder, and they will let the Reitsmas go free." He looked drained, but he had not broken down and he was still calm and dignified.

"Why can't they let us all go free?" I asked, pressing my face against his chest as he comforted me.

He looked down at me and shook his head. "I suppose that is because they think we are the enemy," he said wryly.

At that moment one of the Gestapo officers who had interrogated me entered the room to take Mutti and the Reitsmas away. Mutti told us later that they were driven home and she had led the Gestapo officer up to the bathroom and showed him the large box of talcum powder that stood on the shelf. He undid the bottom of the container, and out fell both the powder and all the jewelry that Mutti had hidden there — a platinum watch, diamond rings, gold and silver bracelets and brooches. It was quite a haul and he seemed satisfied.

Eventually the Gestapo brought Mutti back to the room where Pappy, Heinz and I had been waiting with our arms around each other. They told us that the Reitsmas would be allowed to go free but that we were now going to be transferred to the local Dutch prison.

The Germans need not have kept their word over the deal they made with my parents, but they did. The Reitsmas were left alone after that, and with the help of our secret hoard of food all three of them managed to survive the war. In some respects, amazing though it seems, the Germans behaved honorably.

5

Prison

The black prison van jolted us towards the local jail. We sat in the back with several other families, staring impassively at one another: all of us in deep shock. Dutch prison officers bundled us out of the back and separated the men from the women. I clung to Mutti. She had her eyes on Pappy, who mouthed, "Chin up!" to us as we were marched away from each other.

This was the very worst thing that had ever happened to me. I could not see why I should be put into prison or why, at the age of fifteen, I was such an undesirable person because I was Jewish. It was all a senseless persecution, and I felt very bitter. I wished I knew why this was all happening to us.

When you become caught in such a trap and are powerless to do anything about it, you begin to feel quite empty inside. My normal instincts would have been to involve myself with the people around me and talk to them, but any one of them now could have been the enemy spying us out. There was no one I would trust from now on, except Mutti. Thus began the detachment that was part of the dehumanizing process of the concentration camps.

Mutti and I were ordered into a large dormitory where

there were rows of bunk beds, three beds high. About forty other women were already confined in there, with only the most primitive toilet facilities in one corner. It was the first time I had ever had to share my nights with so many people. I climbed on to a top bunk and lay on top of a grey blanket, my head on a small pillow, staring up at the ceiling. My body ached from the beating I had received. I leaned over to Mutti on the bunk below — I did not want to face the night alone. She nodded as she saw my tousled hair and bruised face looking down at her, and I tipped myself over the side and lay on her bunk next to her. I couldn't sleep at all.

Throughout the night new captives were being brought in. There were women with babies who sensed the distress and screamed with fear while mothers had to cope with their infants without any facilities. There was a chronic asthmatic who suffered several attacks during the night and whose breathing was so ragged that people were screaming out for a doctor and nurses. The Dutch guards eventually sent in a doctor to look at her.

Mutti lay silently and eventually I managed to shut out all the noises and goings-on and slip into a spell of unconsciousness with her arms around me.

The following morning we were given some food. It was the first morsel of bread or liquid that I had tasted since my interrupted birthday breakfast. I suddenly became quite ravenous, and Mutti handed me some of her bread after I had finished mine. While we were sitting on our bunks eating, everyone told each other their stories and how they had been caught . . . and we all tried to guess what our fate was likely to be.

Everybody was quite desperate, but on the bunk next to ours was a young woman in her early twenties who seemed to radiate courage. When morning came, she went around the room, helping the mothers with their babies, comforting crying women and encouraging everyone to keep up their spirits.

Food was brought in again at midday, and she sat next to me on my bunk while we ate. She said her name was Francesca (Franzi) and that she had been born in Amsterdam, although her parents came from Russia. She had expected to enter university the year the Nazis arrived. Despite the fact that her mother had been caught early — together with her older brother and his wife — Franzi and her younger sister, Irene, had managed to go into hiding.

They had taken with them her brother's baby girl, Rusha. Because of the baby, they had had to change hiding places many times with the help of the Dutch underground, but recently Irene and Rusha had been placed on a farm far out in the countryside to live as children of the farmer and his wife. Franzi had been praying that they were still undetected. In the end her own fate had been the same as ours; she too had been betrayed for money.

"At least we are in a proper Dutch prison," she said. "The Dutch are humane, and we are relatively safe here."

By the end of our second day the prison was completely overflowing, and we guessed that we would soon be sent to a Dutch holding camp for detainees away in the country at Westerbork.

"Would it be better to be out there?" I asked, beginning to face the reality that we were captives of our deadly enemy.

Franzi nodded. She had heard of the camp. "It would certainly be less cramped than in here." She looked around at the bunk beds with several women and children sharing. "So long as we're detained in Holland our lives should be safe. They'll let families stay together." She had complete confidence in the Dutch.

Mutti sat silently with her own thoughts and suddenly suggested that she write a quick note to the Reitsmas to bring us some clothing. She went over to the prison guard and negotiated to get a letter sent out. Sure enough, that evening a small suitcase containing some underwear, jumpers, skirts and Mutti's coat was delivered to us in prison.

13 May 1944

On Thursday morning we were all called out by name, lined up and marched to the station under the heavy guard of the Gestapo.

We boarded a normal train with seats and carriages, and as I climbed up I caught a glimpse of Pappy and Heinz on the platform.

A whistle blew and the train rolled away from Amsterdam, picking up speed and rushing through the spring countryside where fruit trees were in full bloom. I could see cows and sheep grazing, farmers working in their fields and I longed to be outside and free.

Inside the carriage we discussed our prospects. We were all afraid that we would be sent on to a concentration camp in the East. Perhaps even Auschwitz. Our only hope was that the war would finish soon and that we could remain in Westerbork till then.

When we eventually arrived, Franzi was proved right. The accommodation there was fairly reasonable. We had clean bunk beds, good toilet facilities and, even better, we were allowed to move around freely to talk to each other and mix with the men during the day. Pappy and Heinz soon found us and stayed close.

We ate in a large dining area together and were given

stamp-pot — mashed potatoes and carrots with gravy poured over them — which tasted good. At the tables everyone had stories to tell.

The detainees at Westerbork were mostly Jews and a few Christians who had sheltered Jews. There was also a group of gypsies, who, to the Nazis, were just as loathsome as the Jews. As new arrivals our group contained the most vulnerable of the detainees. Although the Dutch were the senior adminis-trators under the supervision of Germans, most of the inter-nal running of the camp was performed efficiently by Jews, some of whom Pappy knew personally.

Mutti and he considered our position. "If I can, I will make contact with people here I knew before the war," Pappy said. "Some of them are in influential positions. If they can get us suitable work, we could try to maneuver ourselves into protected positions. That way we might avoid being shipped out." He believed this was our only chance.

He did his best. Some friends recognized him and vowed to do all in their power to help us. We knew the most impor-tant thing was for us to remain in Holland as long as possible.

One of Pappy's friends, George Hirsch, worked in the main office. He promised to try to put us on a work schedule. He was a sincere and kind man. He shared his shirts with Pappy and Heinz because neither of them had a change of clothing.

To our dismay, we began to hear rumors that a large transport of gypsies was to be taken to Auschwitz on the fol-lowing Sunday and as there were still a few cattle trucks to be filled, Jews would be loaded to make up the cargo. Since we were among the newest arrivals, Mr. Hirsch had not had a chance to secure work for us. We felt we were bound to be among the unlucky ones.

We then realized that this was the step into the abyss. Auschwitz was in Poland, far away in enemy territory. We had heard on the BBC that it was known as an extermination camp.

We tried to keep each other's spirits up. Surely as long as we were fit and able to work they would not kill us?

There was little Pappy could do now except give us lectures on survival. He emphasized that caring and fellowship were important, that we would have to help each other to survive. He talked about our need for cleanliness and hygiene. He kept reminding me not to sit on a toilet seat and to wash my hands afterwards. Little did he realize that none of us would have any control over such refinements as these.

Part II

AUSCHWITZ-BIRKENAU

6

Deported

At dawn on Sunday morning, while we were still in our dormitory, a female prison guard appeared and read out a list of names for immediate deportation.

". . . Fritzi Geiringer, Eva Geiringer . . ." Our hearts sank as we heard our names called out. Franzi was also included.

Nervous and upset, we made arrangements to leave. Those remaining were extremely relieved that they had been able to prolong their stay in Holland, but they did as much as they could to supply us with extra food, clothing, blankets, suitcases, even shoes — anything that might aid our survival on the journey and after. Exactly four days after we had visited Pappy and Heinz in their "safe" house we were being deported. We assumed we were on our way to Auschwitz, but in reality we had no idea.

Hundreds of us walked towards the railway sidings. As we made our way to the cattle trucks, carrying our cases and jostling against each other, Pappy and Heinz suddenly appeared close beside me. When I looked around for Franzi, she had disappeared in the crowd.

As we drew nearer to the train, we could see the front part already filled with gypsies — unkempt-looking men and women carrying babies and toddlers, with older children hanging on to their mothers' skirts. Pappy, Mutti, Heinz and I clung together, too, so that we would not be separated. We pulled and pushed each other onto the boards of the truck with little dignity and handed up our cases and blankets. The wagon was so tightly packed that we could not sit down, and we huddled against each other in a corner. Pappy's arms were tight around me, and Mutti held Heinz. The only comfort was that we were still together.

As I looked up, I could see two tiny barred windows near the ceiling of the truck. I also noticed two iron pails standing in the far corner. That was the only provision made for our needs.

Many people from the Westerbork camp had come down to see us off and give us courage. We waited for about an hour until, on a shouted command, the doors were slammed shut and bolted from the outside.

Now there was so little light in the truck that we could hardly see each other's faces. It was like descending into Hell. The wagons shuddered and the cattle train began to move. As the journey went on, people took turns to stand so that others could have a little more space to stretch out on the boards. We did what we could to help one another, but there wasn't much we could do.

During the day the doors were opened once, the buckets changed and some bread thrown in — it was like feeding animals in cages. Several people became violently sick, and that added to the stench and stress in the carriage. Among us was a pregnant woman who was panic-stricken; if she went into labor during the journey, who would help her with her baby?

Each time the doors were opened we tried to communicate with the guards, pleading for compassion and help, but all requests were ignored by the impassive and stony-faced SS men. Vicious dogs barked at us and rifles were pointed into the truck. The impulse to try to escape was very strong, but we knew there was little chance of succeeding. We were unarmed, defenceless civilians and would doubtless be shot in the back if we tried to run away.

When we said anything at all to our captors, the only words spat back at us in German were, *"Halt das Maul, Sau Juden"* ("Shut up, filthy Jews").

At one halt, when the doors were opened, we were faced with machine guns trained against the carriages. Guards shouted at us to hand over all the valuables we still possessed, including wedding rings and watches. They threatened to kill anyone who did not comply. After that stop we did not even know the time.

As the train rolled on, day and night merged. There were two, maybe three days of intermittent traveling. Sometimes we could sense that the train had stopped on a siding where it remained for hours. Without movement the trucks became unbearably hot and airless. The stench from the buckets overpowered us, making many more people feel extremely ill.

After about three days of this existence the train jolted to a halt, and we could hear shouting outside and doors grating open. Violent commands were issued in German. Many could not understand, but I was born in Austria and was nine years old when I left. German was my mother tongue.

As our doors were pushed open, we could see lorries (trucks) waiting next to the train. The SS were shouting, "If there are any ill people or some too tired to walk a long way, they can now go on the lorry to the camp."

With great relief many people climbed down and walked straight over to a lorry, shouting back to their relatives, "We'll see you there!"

The rest of us watched them being driven away. Much later in the camp we learned that these people had been driven directly to the gas chambers.

We could see German guards with guns and dogs, ordering us to get out. There were few guards compared to the many Jews and gypsies, but we were so subdued that we never dreamt of doing anything but obey all their commands. I don't know why. Perhaps we truly thought that our conditions were going to improve. It seemed that nothing could get worse.

Just as I was about to climb down, Mutti handed me a long coat and a grown-up-looking felt hat. "Put this on," she instructed.

"I don't need it," I protested. It was a boiling hot day, and just to be outside in the air would be a relief.

"Put it on," she insisted. "It may be all that you'll be allowed to take in with you. They may take our cases."

At that point more commands came in German. "Get out, put all your belongings next to the train and stand in rows of five."

Very reluctantly I put the coat on. I was sure I looked silly in the hat. It was brown felt and far too grown-up for me. I would never wear such an awful hat by choice.

"You look a smart young lady now," Pappy said, trying to encourage me.

Heinz gave me a weak smile. He looked petrified, his face white with fear as he jumped down from the truck, but he turned to help me. As I sprang down into his arms, I found mine around his neck. Suddenly we were squeezing and hugging each other as if we would never see each other again.

It took about an hour of unloading and organization before the women were ordered to walk towards the front of the platform, while the men were separated and marched towards the back.

Pappy grabbed hold of my hands, looked deeply into my eyes and said, "God will protect you, Evertje."

Mutti clasped Heinz close to her, running her fingers through his hair and kissing his face. Then my parents embraced for the last time before being forced to turn and walk away from each other.

We moved along in lines of five for about ten minutes until we came to a group of SS men. They were dividing the line into right and left. All the old people and children up to about fifteen had to go to the right, while the rest of the women were directed to the left.

Sometimes a mother had to relinquish her young child to an older person who was sent to the right. As we came towards the selectors, the young woman in front of me began first to cry and then to scream wildly as she was forced to give her infant son of eight or nine months into the arms of a stranger, an elderly woman, whose eyes were filled with tears.

"I'll look after him," she said. Her arms were almost too feeble to hold him as he twisted back to grab at his mother.

"I want to go with him!" the mother was screaming out, but she was pulled back roughly. The baby started to howl pitifully.

"I won't recognize him again," she pleaded, trying to calm down and make a reasonable protest. "He's growing so quickly."

The guards looked on impassively.

"Please . . . please don't take my son away!" She began to scream again and tried to grab the baby back while the guard pushed the old woman on and stood between them.

I watched helplessly, but then Mutti stepped forward and put her arms around the sobbing woman's shoulders.

"Even if you don't recognize your baby," she said, "the old lady will remember you and will know who to hand him back to."

This story seemed to pacify her. Her resistance faded, she became quiet and moved on in the line. No matter how much people began to protest or cry, or try to go to the other side to be with their families, it was to no avail. The process was relentless. Thus families were systematically torn apart. At this stage, though, we still did not realize what "selection" really meant.

Then it was my turn. The SS officer looked me up and down and indicated left. Mutti was quickly able to come and stand beside me in line, holding on to my arm. I was only just fifteen. I noticed much later that I was the youngest person by far in our transport line. Many mothers had lost daughters of my age. Ridiculous though it had looked on me, that hat and the long coat had saved my life. Pappy's prayers had once more been answered.

7

Birkenau

The railway track ended at Birkenau near the women's concentration camp. The main Auschwitz men's camp was four or five kilometers away. It was a beautifully hot May day, when spring flowers are at their best, but as I looked around there was nothing growing anywhere in sight, not even a tree or a bush. The whole area was a dried-up desert of barren earth and dust.

Mutti and I walked in line with the other captives. Many Dutch from Westerbork were there and I caught sight of Franzi a little ahead of us. At first we were glad to move forward, stretching our legs without the encumbrance of heavy baggage, but we soon became part of a weary trail of tramping, thirsty women.

After a march of about twenty minutes and in a state of near exhaustion, we reached the gate of the huge compound.

Row upon row of ugly wooden barracks stretched into the distance enclosed by electrified barbed wire higher than a man. Sentries in tall watchtowers overlooked the camp surrounds. We were now defenseless captives, entirely in the hands of the Germans. Even in the heat I shivered.

Once inside the compound we were marshalled into a

barrack to stand waiting for our "reception." And there we waited. We had been without food or drink for more than twenty-four hours. When some women fainted and fell to the ground, no one took any notice of them. I thought it was cruel until I began to envy them. Unconsciousness would have been a welcome relief.

Hundreds of us stood in the airless barrack guarded by only a few German soldiers with rifles pointing at us. After a wait that seemed endless, our "reception committee" eventually appeared: eight women all dressed in striped blue and grey prison uniforms. Their grey faces sneered at us as they walked along our lines.

These women were the Kappos, Polish prisoners of war who were used by the SS to administer the concentration camps. They strode through our ranks, pushing and punching us.

"Welcome to Birkenau," they jeered. "You're the lucky ones, you've only just arrived — we've been here for years. We're in charge here and you will obey our orders. Your luck has just run out!"

A heavily built Kappo moved out in front of us.

"Can you smell the camp crematorium?" she shouted viciously. "That's where your dear relatives have been gassed in what they thought were shower rooms. They're burning now. You'll never see them again!"

We tried not to listen. She was just trying to frighten us. We did not believe her; it was simply too terrible to contemplate.

"You are filthy Jews!" shouted the chief Kappo, "and we are going to delouse you . . . after that you will be tattooed, shaved and clothed."

Mutti stepped forward from the line.

"We are all thirsty. We need water," she pleaded.

She should have known they'd have no time for such a simple request. Their faces, hardened by their own suffering, showed little concern for us — we were new prisoners who had experienced relatively little hardship in the war until now. They ordered her to get back in line, but she began to sway and nearly fainted. She did not fall, however, because we were all pressed very close together. One of the Kappos who seemed a bit kinder came and patted Mutti's face to revive her.

"Don't faint, it's dangerous," she said. "You will get water but not yet." Turning to everyone else, she warned, "Don't drink the tap water. It carries typhus and dysentery."

I stood there in my heavy overcoat and hat, feeling as if I were dying of thirst. My feet were hurting too. I looked down at my dust-covered shoes. Inside them, under my instep, were specially made steel supports that Mutti insisted I wear because I was so flat-footed. I wished I could take them off and sit down.

At last we were herded into a large building with an anteroom where we had to leave any last belongings we possessed, including everything that we wore. I did not want to undress and be naked, but I knew I had no choice. Mutti was undressing and then I saw Franzi doing the same, so how could I protest? As I took my shoes off, Mutti reminded me to keep hold of my metal supports in case they got lost, so I walked along with the rest, all of us completely naked, into a large shower room, carrying my supports with me.

The shower room was a large concrete shell with no windows or cubicles. Along the ceiling I could see pipes capped with nozzles. There were drainage runs and outlet holes in the floor.

As we huddled together and waited, the doors were closed behind us. I thought of the things the Kappos had told us. Were these showers water or gas? I began to shake with fear and Mutti gripped my hand tightly. Suddenly cold water poured down on to our heads.

There were no flannels (washcloths) or soap but the cool water revived me and I began to wash away the last three days of weary traveling. I scooped up a small amount of water and moistened my parched lips. Mutti patted my bottom and smiled at me; her fair hair, now darkened by the water, lay against her head, curling over her ears and at the nape of her neck. I thought how young she looked. I loved her so much.

Eventually the flow of water ceased, doors at the other side of the shower room were thrown open and we were able to walk out. I looked around for a towel but there were none supplied, nor any clothes. Our wet bodies had to steam in the heat of the afternoon.

We were ordered to walk in single file towards a couple of women prisoners who were shaving everyone's hair. All hair was being removed. My pubic hair was soft and new — I had watched it appear over the last two years as I turned into a woman, and now I was going to have to submit to having it shaved off.

"Open your legs," the Kappo ordered.

I was intensely embarrassed as she scraped the razor over my soft skin. I did not see the reason for this humiliation. After that she shaved under my arms, but when she started to cut off the hair on my head with large blunt scissors, Mutti could not resist trying to interfere on my behalf.

She tousled my hair with her hand and said to the Kappo, "She's very young, leave her a little hair on her head!" There was Mutti beginning to take charge! Incredibly the woman complied and left me with an inch of golden spikes framing my forehead.

Mutti smiled at me.

"That looks quite sweet," she said encouragingly.

"Where are your steel supports?" she demanded, just as they were chopping off the hair on her head.

"I must have left them in the shower," I said. They were the last things I had been worrying about.

"Oh, Eva, really!" she said in exasperation, as much with her own condition as mine; she looked strangely unlike my mother as her hair fell away. "How will you manage to correct your bad feet without proper supports?"

"I'll go back and get them," I said, but as I turned I was immediately prevented from moving further by a Kappo with a truncheon, who barred my way and warned me to stand back.

She was directing the line of naked and shorn women to a table at the far end of the room where everyone was being questioned in turn about their names, ages and professions. It was just like being admitted into a hospital. Every detail was written down on a form. This efficiency gave us a sense of being enrolled. As I stood and listened, I noticed that everybody in front of me suddenly seemed to have a useful profession. Ordinary housewives declared themselves to be "cooks" or "dressmakers," "shoemenders" or "nurses," so when I came to give them my details I said I was a secretary.

From time to time SS men came in and strolled around to look and leer at our bodies. It was a sport for them to pinch the bottoms of younger, attractive women, and I felt really degraded when one of the men walked near to me and then pinched my bottom.

We are being treated like cattle — not people, I thought.

We were lined up to be tattooed on our arm with numbers corresponding to those on our admission papers. Mutti was branded first, and when it was my turn, she stood beside me with her arm round my shoulder.

"She is only a child," Mutti said. "Don't hurt her." Once again the woman acquiesced so that the tattoo on my left arm was done as gently as it could be and my number came out much fainter than the others.

All this processing had taken hours. We were very thirsty and feeling faint. I was so thirsty that I promised myself I would drink the first water I saw.

At last we were moved on to the final "reception room" where we were given some clothing. Everybody was issued one pair of knickers (underwear) of indiscriminate size, one overgarment handed out at random and two shoes. Not a pair of shoes, not even a right and left shoe, just two odd shoes. None of them matched, and we spent some time going round to each other trying to swap garments and shoes to fit.

So much for my steel supports! I thought.

As we were about to be let outside, I heard the SS screaming at the Kappo guards. They in turn shouted at us to get back into line. We were all queued up again to be re-tattooed. Apparently, there had been some error in the numbering, and the "clerk" had made a mistake. My number which was A/5232 was changed to A/5272. She simply scored a line through the "3" and tattooed "7" on top, just as I might have corrected mistakes in my exercise book. Even with tattooing everything had to be done exactly by the book.

The ordeal was finally over. We stepped out into the early evening light to be marshalled to our quarters. As we began to move forward in fives, I spied an outside tap on the wall of one of the buildings. I could not resist it. Darting over, I turned on the tap, put my mouth to the stream of water and drank. It was so wonderful to taste that refreshing liquid. Several others copied me and ran over to the tap before we were screamed at and pushed back into line.

It was a weary walk for us in unaccustomed footwear along a dry and dusty road. We stumbled towards the quarantine block where we were to be kept apart from the rest of the camp for the next three weeks. It seemed ridiculous to take such precautions.

Birkenau was the largest of the Auschwitz camps — a vast complex of barrack buildings divided and subdivided by barbed wire and electrified fencing. Some of the buildings had originally been designed as stables; others had been built by former generations of inmates. The entire camp held tens of thousands of prisoners, and the compound we were taken to contained about twenty barracks, each housing approximately 500 to 800 women.

There were two Kappos — barrack bosses — in each building whose task was to administer the block according to Nazi regulations. For the most part they were Polish Christians, though a few were Jews. They survived as long as they were tough enough to control the rest of us. They had special privileges and their own small rooms with stoves at the end of the block where they could cook their own food and keep warm.

We, on the other hand, had no facilities at all. We had to sleep ten to a bed — and a "bed" was one tier of a three-level wooden bunk. That first night, when we were ordered to get into bed, I climbed into a middle bunk with Mutti and eight others. We had not been given any food or water since we had arrived. Even though it was still early evening we were told we had missed supper and would have to wait for breakfast.

I was utterly exhausted. Oblivious to everything, including our bedmates, I lay in Mutti's arms and slept.

In the early hours of the following morning before the sun was up (it was about 4:00 a.m.), the Kappo women appeared and yelled at us to get up and make our beds — even this routine was strictly regimented; the blankets had to be fitted and tucked in absolutely symmetrically. Then we had to sweep the barracks — funnily enough, there was little dirt or rubbish because we had no food or possessions so, while our quarters were relatively clean, it was only we who were filthy and vermin-ridden. Then we were ordered outside for roll call *(Appel)*. It was warm, the sky luminous with a pale yellow light that gradually merged into blue. As we stood in rows of five, I watched the dawn appear. The whole camp was outside waiting to be counted. Every woman prisoner was called out for Appel, in lines along the length of the camp, while German guards and their dogs walked along the rows. The count lasted for two hours. We had to stand without moving, looking straight ahead for as long as it took.

It was to be a test of endurance we would have to face twice every day of our life in the camp. On this warm, summer morning it was inconceivable that we would be subjected to this kind of torture throughout the bitterly cold Polish winter dawns without anything warmer to wear than the clothes we stood up in. Nor did I imagine then that if just one digit of the count was wrong, the whole process would have to begin again. Inevitably, as time wore on into winter, deaths would throw the count out and the ordeal would inflict more deaths the following night.

The first Appel was a special torment because we had still been given neither food nor water. By this time I was so hungry I was desperate for something to eat, but we were not dismissed until the sun was up, and only then were we allowed to return to the barrack where food and drink was distributed. Everyone was given a piece of black bread about four inches thick. Cold black substitute coffee without sugar was handed out in chipped enamel or old tin mugs to one in every five people. As there were not enough utensils to go around, it meant the portion in each mug had to be shared by five. This was the usual system, and we quickly learned that possession of one's own mug was necessary to get one's share. Mutti and I eventually had to sacrifice several rations of bread between us to obtain a mug.

But this morning I hung on to the mug until it was pulled away from me by another desperately thirsty woman. I don't think Mutti had any at all. I ate all my bread immediately without realizing that it was supposed to last for the whole day.

After this feast we were led to the latrines. These were in a barrack five blocks away from ours and consisted simply of an open sewer running down the center of the barrack. Along the middle was a higher stone walk where a supervising Kappo could march the length of the latrines. Each concrete side had about thirty round openings set over the open sewer. There were no facilities for cleanliness or hygiene; no toilet paper, no flushing water and certainly no privacy. As we entered the barrack the stench was overpowering.

One of the golden rules that Pappy had tried to impress upon me was never actually to sit on a strange toilet seat, so I tried to stand — as did several others: we all shared a feeling of intense disgust. However, when the walking Kappo eventually came up behind me, she hit me so hard across my shoulders with her stick that it forced me to sit down. She walked along, striking out with vigor at anyone who tried to stand.

"You will be brought here three times a day in a whole

group," she told us contemptuously, "and you had better use it properly."

And with that, we were marched back to an open courtyard surrounded by barbed-wire fencing outside the perimeter of the barrack and left there to spend the rest of the day.

The sun beat down on our unprotected, newly shaven heads; it burned the backs of our necks and ears and made my fair skin red and sore. There was no shade, nowhere to sit, and nothing to do.

The routine was to be the same for the next three weeks. We were left outside all day, even if it rained. When the skies opened, we were drenched and the dry dust turned into a muddy quagmire around our ankles. We could not avoid being caked in mud and dirt. Every refinement of ordinary human living, even simple shelter, was denied to us. We were being treated like animals — rather worse, because we were not even fed or watered.

We spent the days talking to each other in small groups. Most of us had come from Holland, and since we were sharing the same fate, we tried to become friendly with those around us. We met Franzi again and she joined our little group. She had been through the same ordeal as we had, and although she had not lost her quiet courage, now she seemed to need a little comfort herself.

"Eva reminds me of Irene, my little sister," she said to Mutti, catching hold of my hand and squeezing it. "So we can be a kind of family in here, can't we?"

"Of course," said Mutti. "We will try to take care of each other as best we can."

It was only a token reassurance in such awful circumstances, but from that moment onwards we became trusted friends.

8

Minni

Early on the second day I began to suffer from violent stomach cramps. I had very bad diarrhea and needed to relieve myself almost immediately. I could hardly contain myself as I went to ask the Kappo at the end of the barrack if I could go to the latrines.

"*Verfluchte Mistbiene,** it is not your turn," she spat at me.

"But I have to go!" I was quite desperate.

"You must wait for your turn like everyone else!" she said.

I could hardly believe that she would refuse me, and I did not know what to do. I had terrible cramps that doubled me up, and it was impossible for me to hold on for even two more minutes. I got outside the barrack just in time to crouch down and use a corner of the yard.

But the Kappo had followed me out, and she stormed over, yanked me up and cursed, "You filthy Jew!" She slapped me around the head as hard as she could, yelling, "This is the way you will all die! Infected with dysentery and typhus — because you animals can't control yourselves!"

She had a firm grip on my dress. She dragged me for-

*Literally *Damned shit-bee*

ward, hitting me viciously across my face, first on the right side and then on the left until my ears rang and I felt even sicker than I was already.

"Here is a bad example to you all," she shouted to the others. "Her thoughtless action will give you all contagious illnesses. She is a typical specimen of you pigs and we will punish her!"

Everyone was called out to witness my degradation. I had to fetch a heavy wooden stool, then kneel down and hold it above my head. All the members of the barrack had to stand in a circle around me. As I sank to kneel in the dust, terrible stomach cramps gripped me again.

The heat became unbearable as the sun beat down on my shaven head, severely burning the back of my neck and ears. I was plagued with thirst. My arms ached as I struggled to keep the stool above my head. If I flagged and tried to rest a bit with the seat on my head to release the tension in my arms, the Kappo would come over and kick me. I was in agony.

Mutti had placed herself right in front of me and she was crying; her face showed me her heart was nearly breaking with anguish at the sight of my plight. But as I knelt there in the center of the crowd, they started to whisper encouraging words to support me.

"Come on, Eva!"

"It won't be much longer!"

"Don't give in, Eva!"

But no Kappo was going to have the satisfaction of seeing me do that! Somehow I got through the next two hours until I heard the voice of the Kappo saying, "That will teach you to obey orders in future."

My ordeal was over. Everyone crowded around and made a great fuss of me for having been so brave and tough — even though, they said, I was so young. They supported me, half fainting, back to the barrack, and I was left to lie on the bunk for the rest of the day. By the evening the stomach cramps had gone, and I was feeling much better.

At first I seemed to recover because for a time I became a little heroine and it boosted my morale. Many women yearned so desperately for their own children that they poured all their maternal love on me and I became quite a pet.

However, the ailment had got hold of me. I awoke a few days later shaking with fever, and burning with such a high temperature that I could hardly stand up. But I knew I had to go out on Appel because otherwise the count would not be correct; it would last for hours and it would all be my fault.

My teeth were chattering so much I could hardly speak. "Help me, Mutti," I moaned.

She lifted me against her, supporting me until we were outside. Franzi stayed close by to help hold me up, and we managed to position ourselves in the last row so that when no SS women or Kappos were near enough to see, I could lean against the wall. It was early dawn again. By now I was only semi-conscious. Once or twice I sank on to my heels after Mutti or Franzi told me my head had been counted. Throughout that day I lay in the compound barely conscious of anything around and by the next day I was still no better.

Any inmate with a high fever was a dangerous bunk-fellow. By now the others were beginning to complain that I should not be there. "Take her to the hospital block," they kept nagging Mutti, but I refused to go. Even though I had not yet faced up to the reality of the gas chambers, I had realized that the hospital block housed the most vulnerable inmates for torture and death. There were many rumors going round that patients were being experimented on, often in the most painful and disgusting ways.

"I don't want to die!" I sobbed. "I want to stay with you, Mutti." As long as she was there, she would protect me.

I cried continuously with sickness and fear, but the other prisoners were relentless with their insistence and in some ways they were right.

"You can get medicine there," they argued, "that may save your life — not end it!"

They kept up the persuasion because I looked and felt so ill.

"Do it for us, if not for yourself," said Franzi, to add extra weight to their argument.

So in the end I gave in and agreed to go to the hospital. We all suspected that I had typhus.

Mutti applied to the Kappo, giving her my number and her own number so that she could accompany me. It was the system that if anyone needed to go to the hospital, they would put their number forward in the morning and wait to be called to attend, in turn, block by block. I was still shaking and sweating by the time they came for me but managed the ten-minute walk to the hospital block hanging onto Mutti's arm. I thought I was going to pass out, but I remained conscious enough to stand in line with other women who had turned up for "treatment." We were a sad-looking group of bedraggled and dirty human beings.

Although this "hospital" was simply another barrack building, it looked much cleaner than the others. It had an air of professional efficiency about it. Nurses in white aprons bustled around and there were Jewish doctors in white coats. Medical orderlies wore striped blue and grey prison dress and appeared clean and well-fed. The atmosphere was reassuring.

A nurse finally appeared to take the next patient into the surgery. She was fairly tall, with a sturdy pear-shaped body and a full head of hair. I thought she had the face of an angel. She cut an unlikely figure in that place and among the emaciated forms around her she seemed like an Amazon. She moved with a sense of purpose and was obviously the one in charge.

When Mutti saw her, she suddenly let out a scream. Even in my sickened state I could sense her thrill of excitement.

"Minni!" she shrieked at the top of her voice.

The solid figure of the nurse turned to stare at my mother. "Fritzi!" she yelled in turn as she rushed over to us and threw herself into my mother's arms. They hugged each other tightly, laughing and crying with joy. This was Minni, our beloved cousin from Prague. It was wonderful luck for us that she was there of all places.

Mutti and Minni were like sisters; they had spent many childhood holidays together. Minni had married a famous skin specialist, and although she had been in Birkenau for several months, she had been able to gain considerable protection because of her husband's reputation in treating the Germans for skin disorders — and she had often assisted him in his work.

Minni took me in herself to see the doctor, staying to make sure I got the correct drugs. She agreed with him it was probably an attack of typhus. I was extremely ill, but even so, Minni did not want to see me go into the hospital.

Mutti helped me back to our barrack. That evening as we stood for Appel there were thunderstorms with torrential rain. Mutti later confessed that she had been convinced I would not survive the night. I was burning with fever and delirium. Franzi helped drag and pull me to my place on the bunk where I lay in a drugged sleep with all the humiliations and torture of the past weeks obliterated from my mind.

And then, quite amazingly, when I awoke at dawn for the next Appel, my fever had completely gone. I still felt very weak and wobbly, but I knew I was going to pull through.

Everyone was pleased. Mutti was overjoyed. I told myself that if Pappy knew about my recovery he would be proud of me. He was fanatical about good health. He had no patience for anyone who made a fuss over minor illness. He had always taught me to be brave.

My illness made me appreciate my father's wisdom in the way he had brought me up to be tough and fearless because after that episode I realized my body was capable of recovery, even in the most adverse conditions. From that time on I tried not to make a fuss over unimportant things.

My recovery gave me a new view of life and helped make the unbearable bearable. I told myself that it was now up to me. I was determined to survive the war no matter what they did to me.

By now we were all beginning to grasp the truth about the extermination program and to realize that death lay at the end of the line for us. We came face to face with the reality of elimination during the early days of our three-week quarantine. At Appel one evening a German woman SS guard had appeared holding the hand of an angelic little girl whose long golden curls hung halfway down her back. Her young mother, head shaven and in prison stripes, followed behind as they walked along the lines of standing women. The guard was thoroughly enjoying herself, encouraging the child to count along the rows.

"One, two, three, four and five in a row." The guard repeated in a sing-song voice.

The child skipped happily alongside, trying her best to keep up with the numbering, while we all stood still, heads to the front, hardly daring to move for fear of being beaten.

During the next few days these two made regular appearances at Appel. We speculated among ourselves that the mother was probably the girlfriend of an SS officer, which was why she was getting preferential treatment. We never found out exactly what happened, but, one morning, she and her daughter were no longer there. Nor were they ever seen again in the barrack, and the rumor quickly spread that they had been "selected" — that chilling euphemism for "put to death." We started then to realize how vulnerable we all were.

Now that Mutti had made contact with Minni, I felt a bit more secure. From time to time while we were in quarantine she would visit us with a little extra food — a piece of black bread, a bowl of watery soup, sometimes even a portion of cheese. When she came to see us, we were always so hungry that we ate anything she gave us on the spot, occasionally saving a morsel to give to Franzi. We had discovered that saving food for later was useless because it was invariably stolen while you were sleeping or off guard. Everyone was always hungry. Neither the black coffee substitute nor the watery soup had much nutritional value, especially when shared between five. Mutti and I agreed that we would exchange some of the food Minni gave us for our own mugs.

Several inmates had noticed Minni giving us extra food and hung around, hoping for a share. In fact, there was a good deal of extra food around but not for Jews. Polish prisoners were allowed food parcels from home or the Red Cross. Sometimes they would get some bacon or cheese or a bag of sugar. I was desperate for something sweet to eat.

One morning on my way back from the latrines I saw something white and glittering on the ground.

It's sugar, I thought, bending down and pushing my finger into the tiny white particles. I wetted my finger so that I could pick up every tiny little grain. It was the first sweet thing I had tasted for weeks.

9

"Canada"

Towards the end of our quarantine the Kappos told us the SS would be coming to sort us out for different work units. Everyone became very nervous as we realized that our fate was about to be decided.

During the next early Appel a group of five smartly uniformed officers arrived at the camp. They were quite polite to us as they walked up and down the rows of standing women, calling out the names of different work units to a Kappo who took note of each prisoner's tattoo number and the work unit to which she had been allocated. It was very efficiently organized. Unfortunately, we had no idea what the code names represented or to what kind of work we were being sent. We only knew that some units were more desirable than others.

I stood facing straight ahead, looking as bright as I could, feeling the SS coming nearer until they were in front looking me over. Quite suddenly, I did not feel afraid. I looked them squarely in the eyes as the senior officer called out "Canada."

I knew this was an elite work unit because everyone in our compound said they wanted to work there. Completely innocent of the ways of camp protocol I blurted out, "Can my mother come too?"

The Kappo stared at me in disbelief, but the German officer seemed amused.

"Which is your mother?" he asked in a very reasonable tone.

I turned and pointed Mutti out to him. I watched him stroll up to her and, just as a buyer of a horse would look over the animal, turn her around, move her head from side to side and examine her from all angles. Then he nodded and said, "Yes! Why not?"

Mutti and I exchanged relieved glances. We felt that we were beginning to get the hang of manipulating our fate rather better than we had thought possible.

At that point there was a commotion outside the camp. We could hear dogs barking wildly and sounds of shooting. Someone had attempted to escape. We could hear SS running backwards and forwards shouting instructions to each other. Kappos were summoned and we were left standing in our rows. Within the hour, gallows were erected and all of the inmates were summoned to witness the hanging. It was to be an example to us. The escapee, who was a slightly built woman with a shaven head, was dragged forward. She was dishevelled and her feet were bare. Her hands were bound behind her back and there were bloodstains on her dress. Mutti tried to stand in front of me so that I would not see what was going on. But although it was happening before me and although I was forced to look, I did not really see it. None of us saw the hanging. We were forced to look — but we did not see.

Even after this, there was always someone trying to run away. Each morning after Appel when prisoners were taken outside the camp to various places of work, the desire to escape was very strong. Armed guards patrolled with their dogs ready to chase and pull down anyone moving out of line. I really believed that no one could ever get away.

I was afraid most of the time, but occasionally hope rose inside me despite our awful situation. After being allocated to work units, six of us were taken to one side and given the privilege of wearing a striped prison dress. Then we were lined up with 400 or so workers allocated to "Canada." As we walked through the gates, I was uplifted by the sense of freedom.

"This is quite an adventure!" I whispered to Mutti.

We left the camp preceded by a little band playing marching music. We were all dressed alike, but presentably, so that farmers in their fields would not think we were badly treated. However, they must have been aware of the armed guards and dogs that accompanied us, seen our shaven heads and the gaunt, strained faces of the older inmates. Too many of us appeared half-starved for them not to be aware that something horrible was happening to us. But, as most people do when confronted by things they don't want to know about, they turned the other way.

The sun beat down on our bald heads as we marched along towards the sorting camp that was known as "Canada" — a slang name given because this was the land of plenty. It was a huge, open compound, encompassing many sheds and covered areas erected to house the spoils brought in from the trains that shunted prisoners to their deaths. Each morning lorries collected all the remaining personal possessions of the condemned from the railway platform and dumped them here to be sorted by work parties like ours.

We could see huge piles of clothing, great mounds of shoes waiting to be sorted and one heap, taller than my head, of metal and glass. As I drew nearer, I saw it was made up of thousands of pairs of spectacles. It still did not dawn on me why they were no longer needed by their owners.

Mutti and I, with dozens of others, were put into a massive shed where we were each given a pair of scissors. We had to undo the linings of fur coats — hundreds of them — to look for any hidden jewelry, gold, money or anything else that might be there. We found so many things hidden away that, at first, it was a bit like opening a pile of presents.

We would exclaim loudly over items we discovered, especially if we came across biscuits or sweets. We grabbed and ate more or less what we wanted and no one stopped us.

We worked in a relaxed atmosphere, because everyone was eagerly searching for and finding many items of value. Some older inmates kept back small pieces of jewelry, like diamond rings, which they dug into the ground under their feet, hoping they would be able to retrieve them later. It all seemed very enjoyable until I suddenly thought of the people who had kept such precious things in their fur coats, and particularly when I came across photos of babies and their smiling parents. Sometimes these were the only "precious" items hidden away, and it made me very sad.

As I gazed at a photo of a Barmitzvah boy surrounded by his smiling, loving family, the shed seemed to spin around me and I was hit by the enormity of what I was doing. Suddenly I knew that none of these people would ever see each other again, only in heaven. I was paralyzed by the horror of it and at the same time angry that I had allowed myself to enjoy something so hideous and ghastly.

Every evening the workers returned to the barracks to stand for hours at Appel to make sure no one had succeeded in escaping during the day. Inevitably, separation from loved ones, starvation and dehumanization were completely unbearable for some women. I am sure they realized in their hearts that escape was futile, but they made one last-ditch effort to be free before sacrificing their lives. Sometimes they would run out of the marching line outside the camp and be shot in the back or brought down by the dogs and torn to pieces. Or, when they were back inside the camp, they would throw themselves against the barbed wire which was highly electrified. They would scream horribly as they burnt to death on the wire.

Imprisonment was something one had to bear for oneself. If we had been given a chance to survive the conditions, I should have looked on it as an exciting challenge, but I realized that, just like a bull in a bullfight, we did not have a fair chance. The system was designed to kill us all. But my will to live was strong, and I had made a pact with myself that I would try to overcome every challenge.

On returning to camp from "Canada," we suffered the indignity of being physically searched in case we tried to smuggle anything back. We had to open our mouths, take off our shoes and occasionally we had to strip completely. Despite this, people at the camp begged us to smuggle food back for them. Mutti and I often risked discovery and somehow managed to secrete a biscuit or sweet for Franzi and one or two of our friends.

Minni too made a request.

"Fritzi, be a darling," she sighed. "I have such a yearning for a silver spoon. Can you try to bring one back for me?"

Minni came from a wealthy family in Prague and detested having to use the rusty spoons and chipped mugs considered good enough for the inmates of Auschwitz.

Mutti raised her eyebrows and pursed her lips. "It's risky," she said, thinking it over. "But I have an idea that might work."

It took some days before I found a beautifully patterned silver spoon that I knew Minni would appreciate. On Mutti's instructions I slipped it under the instep in my shoe — just like my supports! We felt so daring. My pulse was racing as we entered the camp. I was ready to brazen it out somehow. But luck was with us. The search that evening was cursory and quick and I was able to walk into the camp without detection. When we handed her the spoon that evening, Minni was delighted and we were all pleased with ourselves for having been so clever. Subdued though we were by the hideous regime, we had proved that we had not given up. It was an important victory.

Afterwards I reflected that it had been the most stupid thing to do because we three had such privileged positions. If we had been found out, as some were, we would have been severely punished. It could even have cost us our lives.

6 June 1944
D-Day

The Kappos must have suspected me because soon after the spoon incident I was transferred away from Mutti to another sorting hut. This time it was the bedding department where piles of beautiful handmade patchwork eiderdowns were stacked along one side of the wall. We were instructed to search over every square inch of each one with our fingers and if we felt anything other than soft down we were to tear them apart and retrieve any hidden items sewn inside. We found lots of cigarettes neatly stitched into separate patches, the eiderdown hiding the bulk of the packets. There were gold watches, purses filled with gold coins, precious jewelry and important medicines that people could not live without and had hidden in their quilts for safety.

We were allowed half an hour's break in the middle of the day for food, which was black bread, with cheese or jam confiscated from the latest batch of incoming prisoners. If we wanted, we could sit outside in the sun to eat. One lunchtime I was squatting by myself, my back against the barrack wall munching my ration and idly watching a group of male prisoners passing on the other side of the barbed wire when I suddenly recognized a familiar figure. It was my father!

10

Reunion

I jumped up shouting "Pappy!" He looked at me with such amazement and delight that we wanted both to laugh and cry at the same time. We ran to the barbed wire that separated us. We could almost touch each other, but we did not dare to because it was far too dangerous. We were intoxicated with excitement at the coincidence of seeing one another. In that vast camp we knew it was a miracle for both of us to be in that particular place at the same time. God had brought us together for only a little while, but for ever after I felt I had not been deserted. I kept remembering how it was that suddenly, out of the blue, Pappy was there again. It strengthened my faith and my determination to pull through.

The sight of my dashing, attractive father dressed in striped prison uniform with a beret covering his shaven head was terrible. I knew how fastidious he was about his appearance. He had always had his suits made for him in London's Savile Row. I hated this humiliation and wanted to cry inside, but he was beaming at me and whispered across the barriers, "Evertje, *Liebling.* Thank God you're alive."

"Pappy —" I couldn't say anymore.

"Where's Mutti, is she with you?"

"She's here in 'Canada,' too," I said. "Where's Heinz?" I asked, hoping he was nearby.

"He's alright," Pappy said. "He's on an outside job. Fresh air and exercise are doing him good. I'm working as office manager in a timber factory near here. I'm respected by the workers and even the SS bosses seem impressed. I'm making myself indispensable."

I was sure he was going to be alright.

"Darling, can you get hold of any cigarettes?" he went on more urgently.

"But you don't smoke!" I was surprised he had changed his habits even in prison.

"No, of course not, but they're very useful currency in here. I can exchange them for favors. I might be able to arrange to come again tomorrow — at the same time. Can you be here too?"

I promised I would try, this time with Mutti.

IT WAS WONDERFUL to tell her that night about the meeting and see her face when she knew Pappy and Heinz were still alive and well. We cried with relief.

Somehow, we managed to be by the barrier when Pappy came next day. I watched the reunion of my dear parents as they stood looking at each other on opposite sides of the wire, and I wiped away the tears that trickled down my cheeks with the back of my hand.

Over the next few days Pappy appeared regularly, and Mutti and I were able to throw him packets of cigarettes over the barbed wire. Sometimes we were spotted by the Kappo. A guard even saw us once and gave us a warning, but not too seriously. Everyone else was filching cigarettes too.

By the end of the week to our great disappointment

Pappy was no longer among the men who passed by on the other side of the electrified fence.

Work in "Canada" was dirty and hot, so after our work we were allowed to have a shower before going back to our night barrack. The showers were set up in an open space surrounded by a wooden fence. When we had stripped, many SS men enjoyed themselves by looking over the fence and leering at us. Sometimes they would goad each other into entering the enclosure to play around with the women and splash us with water. Some of the older, wiser inmates warned me time and again that I would have to be very careful not to get caught by a German and pulled into a corner to be raped. I was more scared of this than anything else, so I tried to keep safely hidden. For a while, I managed to edge away from their sight by standing behind someone larger than me.

But one young soldier kept eyeing me. He began to follow me, stalking me around the camp. Everywhere I went I noticed him watching me — in the compound, in the showers, everywhere. I tried to go around in groups for protection, but I knew he was becoming a particular threat to me.

One afternoon a Kappo called me out to take a message from one shed to another. As I left I was horrified to see this soldier walking after me. He had a rifle slung over his shoulder, and his footsteps sounded deliberate and determined. I was petrified. I did not know what to do. He could easily overpower me, and if I resisted he might kill me.

"Please God, help me!" I prayed fervently, half-running, half-walking to keep in front of him, when I saw an enormous heap of clothing, about ten meters high, that had been dumped there for sorting. Several women were grouped around talking and gesticulating, so I quickly scurried behind them and buried myself deep inside the mountain of clothes.

I was certain that no one had spied me, and I prayed that when I eventually came out the soldier would be gone.

I could hear the sorters talking among themselves as they gradually reduced the proportions of my hide-out, but I dared not risk them seeing me since they might give me away. I stayed hidden for what seemed ages — at least half an hour. All began to go quiet outside as the sorters moved away. I realized that if I stayed there much longer I would get a beating from the Kappo, so, very slowly and cautiously, I pushed my shaven head out from under the overcoats and dresses and warily looked around.

To my enormous relief the soldier had given up and gone. My luck was still in. I chuckled at the thought of how comical I must have looked with my egg-head gradually emerging from a heap of clothing.

Our "good" life lasted for a very short time, only a few weeks, throughout June and into July. Inevitably our luck was beginning to run out.

In June thousands of Hungarians had arrived as prisoners, and workers in "Canada" labored at top speed sorting out their possessions for the Nazis; I still looked out for Pappy daily but he did not come.

By the end of July, there was a diminishing intake into Auschwitz and we were laid off.

20 August 1944
Russians capture Rumania

There was no other constructive work for us to do, so Mutti and I were transferred to another sort of work, the Aussen Komando.

We were put with a group of women who had to carry

huge blocks of stone from one side of the camp to the other. Then, to fill in the time, we had to chip away at the stones with heavy hammers and break them down into tiny pieces. This interesting work was supervised by the more brutal Germans. They were vicious bullies. If we dared to rest a little or did not hit the stones hard enough, they would curse us, threaten us with the butt of a gun and finally beat us up. We suffered hard labor for several weeks, by which time Mutti had become very thin, partly from lack of food but also from exertion and worry.

Sometimes in the evenings we had the rare relief of a spare twenty minutes between work and Appel. It was then Mutti had an idea to augment our diet.

"Let's go behind the kitchen barrack and see what we can find on the rubbish heap," she said.

We made sure that nobody realized what we were up to as we walked nonchalantly along the blocks until we came to the stinking waste stacked behind the kitchen. Mutti kept lookout while I picked up a discarded carrot top.

"This must be good to eat," I said as I gnawed at it.

"I could try and swap that part," said Mutti, looking at the wizened green stalk and leaves. "I could say it is vitamin-rich parsley."

I rummaged around and discovered half a moldy pumpkin with some flesh clinging to the inside.

"We could pretend this is melon," I said.

We put small pieces of discarded peel and the green carrot tops into our mugs and carried them back to our barrack. We called them melon and parsley and exchanged them for bread. Everyone craved extra vitamins. We knew it was essential to try to keep our strength up. It was becoming a matter of life and death for all of us. We wanted to prevent the swol-

len legs and bellies that lack of vitamins had produced in lon-
ger-term prisoners.

Taking it in turns to be lookout, we tried to scavenge in
the waste bins as often as possible for beet-ends, onion skins,
cabbage leaves — anything that we could eat with our bread as
a little extra delicacy. Mutti made me wash the pieces of discarded vegetables in our substitute coffee to avoid infection.

Wherever we walked we scanned the ground for anything
useful. One evening when we were wandering miserably
around the compound Mutti discovered some waste buckets
full of little items like hankies, scarves, gloves, even cigarettes. These were small personal belongings that the new arrivals had kept in their pockets until they had finally been
forced to throw them away. For us they were riches. We took
what we could. The hankies were dirty, of course, but we
washed them as best we could in the showers, folded them
neatly and dried them under the mattress. Then we walked
through the block calling out, "Who wants to swap bread for
hankies, scarves or cigarettes?" and got more offers than we
had goods.

It was an extraordinary way to start a little business but it
worked. Occasionally we were found out and punished — our
own bread ration was confiscated — but we became quite
sought after by women who had something to swap. In the
evenings we talked incessantly among ourselves about food.
By now we were all much thinner and lethargic. We noticed
the physical change in all of us. Oddly enough, almost from
the first week, not one of us had our periods. We were worried
about what would happen if we did have a period, especially
as we had nothing to keep us clean, but we never had one.
Someone said there was bromide in the soup which stopped
them, but we didn't know if that was true. I felt it might be

the case because I often had a strange sense of "floating" after drinking the soup.

25 August 1944
Paris liberated

Every few weeks our hair would be cropped to our skulls by the Kappos who wielded large blunt scissors. It was painful and humiliating. Mutti's head looked very strange and knobbly after it was shaved. She was always grateful when her hair had grown a couple of centimeters and began to cover her skull again. She said she felt more human. The Kappos insisted that having our heads shaved regularly was to control lice. It was, in fact, a deliberately dehumanizing process that made us look and feel like criminals. We hated having to submit to it.

3 September 1944
Brussels liberated by British forces

2 October 1944
US First Army breaches Siegfried Line north of Aachen

At the beginning of October, during the weekly shower sessions, we noticed a difference in the atmosphere. Something awful was about to happen. The Kappos were shouting at us more than usual. Fear hung in the air.

As always we left our clothes outside before showering. We were very frightened as we entered the shower room and heard the doors close behind us. We held our breath. When cool water streamed down on our heads, we prayed with relief.

But to our dismay, as the doors opened on the other side

to let us out, there stood several SS men and women. A slim, upright and immaculately uniformed officer stood in front of them facing us. We immediately recognized him as Dr. Mengele, who held the power of life or death over us. He was known as Dr. Death. The stories of his appalling experiments circulated among the prisoners and brought terror to his victims. We realized with intense fear that a "selection" was to be held.

Each one of us had to take part in a desperate parade where we had to turn slowly around in front of him. He scrutinized us with a kind of clinical precision to decide our fate. We all tried to stand upright and look strong, but we were a pathetic group of undernourished, overworked and emaciated women. At his indication the first few were sent to the right, then one little woman was sent to the left. She stood there trembling with fright. Soon another two were sent to her side where they stood clinging together. The sorting continued.

When I walked forward, he waved me to the right. I turned to wait for Mutti but was horrified to see a Kappo push her roughly over to the selected side.

I screamed. Mutti rushed across the room to give me a farewell kiss, but one of the SS women caught her and beat her fiercely over the spine with a leather belt, but not before she had managed to get near enough to me to give a whispered instruction.

"Try and tell Minni!"

My body started to shake uncontrollably, and my teeth chattered violently as I watched my mother, my darling Mutti, being marched away naked with others in her group. It was the blackest moment of my life. I thought it was the last time I would ever see her.

II

Alone

We dressed in grim silence. That night, instead of being returned to our old barrack in A Lager, we were walked across to another part of the camp which was separated by a barbed-wire gate guarded by a sentry and searchlights.

Franzi tried to comfort me but I was inconsolable. I just knew that I had to try to get to Minni to tell her what had happened. This compulsion was so strong that I did not consider what would happen to me if I got caught.

I told Franzi I was going to go back. She did her best to stop me, pleading and warning, but nothing she said made any sense to me except that if I got killed I would share Mutti's fate.

We were herded onto our bunks once more, and I lay awake, waiting until the middle of the night. Franzi, who was beside me, kissed my head as I slipped off the middle bunk and crept out of the barrack. I could see the sentry tower and I clung to the wall, in the shadows, as the beam of the searchlight swung slowly clockwise over the camp. All was quiet. I moved stealthily towards the sentry gate without considering that it might be shut. By some miracle it was wide open, but I didn't spare it a thought as I ran through, just as the searchlight shone behind me.

I made my way to Minni's barrack and slipped inside. Everybody was asleep. The bunks for the nurses were near the door, and I woke up the first person I came to.

"I've got to see Minni urgently," I whispered.

The sleeper was awake in seconds and whispered back, "Where have you come from? Who are you?" She was off her bunk by now, peering at me to make sure I was not an informer.

"Please, please, it is very important," I insisted. "I have to see Minni."

Several other nurses and patients were awake by now, scared of the commotion I was making. She took hold of my arm and led me down a few lines of bunks until I saw Minni's bulk under a thin blanket. I shook her.

"Eva!" she awoke with a start. "What's the matter?"

She held me to her bosom as I sobbed uncontrollably and blurted out the terrible news. "They have selected Mutti."

"Shh, darling, I will see what I can do. I will try," she repeated, "I will try." I also told her that I had been moved from A Lager to B Lager. Now that I had done all I could, I was beginning to calm down.

"I will speak with Herr Doctor Mengele tomorrow." Minni's tone reassured me. "Go back now. Be very careful that you are not seen."

We kissed each other good-bye, and I made my way back into the night. No one spied me and surprisingly there were no dogs about. When I returned from my perilous crossing, Franzi was waiting by the door to grab hold of me and hug me. I felt limp and numb and crept back into my space on the middle bunk, emotionally and physically exhausted. All the women sharing my bunk, together with some Dutch friends who had known Mutti from our original transport carriage, were wide awake and waiting up for me. They all tried to give me comfort and some hope, and at last I managed to fall asleep.

For the first time since we had been captured I was without Mutti in the night.

The following dawn, after Appel, we were told that we were to be moved to Camp C, about two kilometers away, to another work unit called the Weberei. We were then led away from familiar horrors to unknown ones.

I was in despair. I cried all the way. Franzi walked along beside me, but she could do nothing to stem my tears. I felt that this was the final good-bye and that the last ties with my family — my mother and my cousin — had been broken. Nothing could console me in the knowledge that I was now totally alone.

On that first morning after Mutti's selection, we were marched to a huge shed which contained long trestle tables piled high with heaps of rags and rolls of very hard paper. Our task was to tear the material into ribbons about three centimeters wide, plait them into ropes some five centimeters thick and daily complete a length of twenty meters. We were told that it was going to be cut into meter lengths for throwing hand-grenades. There were only a few pairs of scissors in the entire shed which we could borrow from one another, but mostly we had only our bare hands to use as tools. I often had to use my teeth.

Throughout the day the SS women and men walked round to check that the plaited ropes were strong enough. They were very strict about quality. If you didn't make your plait properly and it came apart when they pulled it, you were thoroughly beaten. Each evening our individual quantity of rope was measured. At first, if we did not complete our lengths, we were warned to do better. If we did not improve, we were told that we would be selected. Inevitably some women were too weak to work properly. Gradually they lost the strength to tear the thicker material with their hands or teeth. One by one, they were selected and they disappeared from the assembly line. We all feared that this would happen to us too, but I always managed to complete my quota.

Now that Mutti was gone my nights were intensely miserable, and without her comforting arms around me I found it very difficult to bear the appalling conditions. Everyone near me somehow tried to show me a little extra love to make up for it, and Franzi made it her business to stay as close to me as she could. That way she remained one of my sleeping partners, and she did her best to stand in for Mutti by cuddling me at night. However, we were all becoming dispirited, worn out with worry and lack of proper food, and no one could take the place of my mother.

All the conditions in the new camp, including the sleeping arrangements, were exactly as before. However, apart from Franzi, I now had a new selection of sleeping partners — we did not have any choice, we were simply allotted places as we marched into the barrack. The others on my bunk were a mixed bunch: some were much older than me; some were intellectuals who found the degradation extremely difficult to cope with; others were rough diamonds, able to accept the conditions — like Gretl, who was also Viennese, and even in this grim situation could always find something to make us smile. But as the youngest I felt very vulnerable and sorry for myself. I was trapped in the most appalling place and at night I dreamt about escaping, running through forests, hiding from my hideous tormentors. I didn't want revenge on the

Kappos. I just wanted to run away from them. I was determined to live, and to be free.

Every night was another test of endurance. No matter what we had been before capture — doctors, nurses, housewives or market women — we were now all in the same predicament. At night we had to be a team. We were so tightly packed on the bunk that no one was able to lie on their back or their front, only on their side. The ten of us slept together like a set of human spoons, so that when one person turned in their sleep we all had to turn. Even our sleep was regimented.

I was normally so tired I couldn't stay awake, even though another kind of bedfellow lay with us — hideous, large, black bedbugs that multiplied freely, flourishing in our warmth and in the old wood of the bunks.

Each time the "team" on the bunk above turned, these revolting bugs dropped down on us in great lumps and stuck to our skins. They were sickening bloodsuckers that feasted off our bodies. There were so many that we would have been covered with them had we not scraped them off immediately. Even so, our skins were pitted with bites and boils from their attacks.

The way we had to live was disgusting. One day I thought I had found a possible remedy for the problem of not being able to clean myself after going to the latrines. I saw a large roll of white cotton wool lying behind a barrack, and I pulled a piece off the roll and kept it safely in the pocket of my dress until I could use it later in the day. I was looking forward to wiping my bottom with something soft, but when I used it I discovered at once it was not cotton wool at all but fiber glass. I had razed my whole backside with tiny fragments of glass splinters which I had to pick out as best I could. It rapidly turned septic and I was sore for days.

One night I was woken by a peculiar sensation on my feet. I looked down to see a black rat about to gnaw at my flesh, and I screamed in fright, making so much noise that people thought I was being killed. I lay there trembling and sweating for a long time until the others in the bunk finally convinced me that the animal had gone. After that incident I dreaded going to sleep.

We suffered daily from hunger pains. There was always just enough food to keep us alive but no more. We were being torn apart by the need for more nourishment. We became so obsessed by food that we could have committed any crime to obtain extra rations. We were often issued with such revolting, moldy gruel that, although I was slowly starving to death, I could not bring myself to eat more than a mouthful of the stuff.

Some days I would volunteer to help fetch the heavy soup vats from the kitchen barracks. These were huge wooden containers, larger than dustbins. It took four of us to stagger back to the hut with them. Very occasionally we were lucky to find them filled with milk. For a minute or two we would manage to set the vat on the ground, out of sight of the barrack, and then drink our fill of the nourishing liquid and thank God for it. We had to be extremely careful not to leave any sign of the theft on our faces or clothes, or we would have suffered a cruel beating from the Kappos.

Because of bugbites and the filthy conditions, I developed a huge boil on the back of my neck. It was drawing together painfully into a great lump that needed to be lanced. There was one particularly vicious Kappo who was always hitting me during Appel because I found it impossible to stand still for such a long period. This time when she struck out at me her hand landed squarely on my boil. That did the trick!

The boil burst open and pus spattered all over her hand and face. I felt great satisfaction in seeing her look of disgust as she wiped it away.

We had learnt early on that it was essential to have a utensil of our own for food, preferably a mug or bowl for the sloppy soup, and in the first weeks Mutti and I had gone without bread in order to swap for one for each of us. We also realized that these old rusted mugs were precious items that were invariably stolen if you took your eyes off them. I usually managed to tie mine around my waist with a rag or piece of string, but even so there were times when I lost my mug and had to starve myself once more to get another. The weekly showers meant that all our clothes were removed for delousing. Nothing belonged to us personally, and if we did have something to make life a little more civilized — like a mug, or a pin, or a piece of soap — then it was often lost with our clothes at the door to the showers. We began to devise ways of keeping them.

The Kappos had sharp eyes and punished anyone they caught holding on to something precious. As I walked past them to the showers with the other naked women, I developed the knack of holding my mug in front of me, then behind me.

It was a terrifying game because of the chance of discovery and the beatings that might follow. Still, our little possessions meant such a lot to us that we set out to hoodwink the Kappos if we possibly could. We would conceal things under our armpits or in even more ingenious ways. One formerly buxom woman, whose ample breasts had now been reduced to thin flaps of empty skin, tried to smuggle a small piece of towelling under her breast-fold. Just as she was about to enter the showers, the Kappo's alert eye detected a minute corner of rag peeping out. She strode over to the culprit and, with a twisted look on her face, grasped hold of the nipple with her thumb and forefinger, lifted up the flap of skin and let the tiny piece of towel drop to the floor. We all stood frozen with fear. There was absolute silence as we waited for the screams of abuse, but the Kappo suddenly saw the comical side of it and fell about laughing. To our relief that incident was over.

After the showers a different set of deloused clothes was thrown at us. If we were lucky, we found small items in the pockets which we could swap. Can you imagine exchanging a rusty safety pin to keep your knickers up, for a scrap of rag to dry yourself? Every tiny item was precious currency.

To feel clean again was a relief but it lasted only a short time. We were plagued by lice. These pests crawled all over my body, they bit me behind the ears, between my legs, on any part of the skin that was moist and warm. Everyone was tormented by them. Although the barracks were clean, we ourselves were filthy and our physical condition encouraged the lice to multiply. Their bites would come up in little blood bumps that burst when we scratched them, but they itched so much that we could not help scratching — it nearly drove us mad. Once a week after showers we were sprayed with some kind of powder that probably killed the living lice but not the eggs, so that a few days later we were crawling with them again.

Every night the bedbugs would renew their attack. Towards the middle of October, when I had managed to get my tin mug through the showers once more, I carefully placed it as usual within eye-sight and hand-reach on the edge of my bunk, before I fell into an exhausted sleep. The night was humid and uncomfortable. When I awoke in the morning and reached out to check that my mug was still in place, it was covered inside and out with a living crust of bedbugs about two centimeters thick. As I grasped the mug my fingers crunched into them and their blood spurted all over my hand. I shuddered with revulsion. It made me want to be sick. So did the incident that happened a few mornings later.

Every night the two toilet buckets at each end of the barracks were used continuously. Anyone who was unlucky enough to get to the buckets and find them already full was compelled to take them to the toilet block to empty them. That meant you had to walk ten blocks with buckets overflowing with excrement. This dreadful task was, of course, left by everybody until the last possible minute when the buckets were full to the brim, and very often it was I who had to carry this revolting load. I would struggle along trying to avoid spilling any over my feet. The buckets were so heavy that you had to be very strong to carry them. The weaker women were unable to get very far, so they would sometimes secretly empty the contents outside, near to our block.

On this particular morning, a German SS woman had noticed the mess on the ground outside. She stormed into the barrack just as we were waking up.

"*Verfluchte Mistbienen!* Can't you even carry your own shit where it belongs?" she screamed at us.

Then she grabbed hold of my mug and shovelled up the contents from the bucket nearby, throwing it over as many of us as she could. The filth landed all over my skirt and legs, and I knew there was no way of cleaning myself until the end of the week. We were left stinking until the next shower.

That was when I felt the greatest kind of despair and degradation. I winced inside as I thought of Pappy and all his good advice about keeping clean. I was powerless against the sadistic treatment of the Kappos. Nothing made me feel more truly alone and frightened.

24 October 1944
Aachen captured by US First Army

Feeling totally deserted, I was now losing the courage and hope that had kept me alive. I knew I had lost Mutti and I longed desperately for Pappy. I needed someone to encourage me to live; without loving help, I could not fight on for survival. I was full of self-pity. I was too young to be left on my own. There was no one I wanted to talk to or confide in. Everyone around me seemed so much older than I was. Even Franzi, who was twenty-five, seemed ancient to me.

Before this time I had been driven by a consuming urge to survive, a spirit fuelled by my close bond with Mutti, my need to live for her sake as well as my own, and by the early training in survival I had received from Pappy. Now I began to realize I could no longer cling to the past. Even if I were to survive, I could not envisage any kind of future for myself. I didn't see how I could cope in a world without my family.

And so, suffering the horrors of the present and seeing no hope in the future, I began to resign myself to death.

12

Pappy

I sat at the bench for fourteen hours a day, hungry, cold and lonely, working on my quota of plaits. I became acutely depressed and often cried — though I rarely spoke. I cut out all thoughts except black ones.

At about ten o'clock one morning a Kappo entered the workroom; she seemed to be looking around for somebody. We were deadly scared. Often when someone was picked out it was because they had done something wrong and were about to suffer immediate punishment or even death. The Kappo strolled up and down the workshop searching the rows of frightened faces, and when I felt her standing behind me, I froze with fear. Though I kept my head down, my hands were shaking so much that I could hardly continue with the plaiting. I waited to feel a heavy blow across my back but, to my utter astonishment, she spoke in a tone quite out of keeping with what I had come to expect from Kappos.

"Go outside," she said in a friendly voice. "There's someone to see you."

I simply could not imagine who would ever come to see me and I was terrified. Perhaps I had caught the eye of an SS man who wanted me for sex? I was extremely unwilling to move, but she insisted and kept prodding me in the back saying, "Hurry up now!"

Slowly and reluctantly I shuffled outside in my ill-fitting shoes, my eyes cast down — I did not dare to look up at the person who was waiting for me. When I finally lifted my head, I could hardly believe my eyes.

"Pappy!" I cried. There he was, dressed in a striped blue and grey prison suit with a beret on his shaven head. He looked very thin and much older than I remembered him, but his eyes were full of an immense love for me. I threw myself into his arms and felt his warmth and strength flow into me and pull me back to life.

I wanted to whoop with joy but instead I burst into tears. I sobbed uncontrollably while he held me close to him as if he would never let me go. He must have felt as happy as I did, to have his little daughter in his arms once more.

At last he pushed me slowly from him. "Evertje, don't cry," he said. "Everything will be alright. Where is Mutti? I will try and see her too."

And then I had to tell him. My body was shaking with anguish as I cried out, "Oh Pappy! She has been selected and gassed!"

He reeled backwards as if I had hit him. He tried not to break down in front of me but his eyes filled with tears and I could see that his world had been destroyed.

He managed to pull himself together for my sake and talked to me quietly but insistently. He told me to be brave and not to give up. "We'll soon be free, Evertje," he promised, squeezing me tightly, "and we will be together again. You, me and Heinz."

"How is Heinz?" I said. I had not dared to ask about him before.

"He's fine," Pappy said. "He's working in the vegetable gardens growing tomatoes. The fresh air and exercise are doing him good."

I was sure he was lying.

"And you should see how tall he has grown," Pappy went on.

There was nothing I wanted more!

"I have a good job," he said, trying to reassure me. "I'm still in charge of the office in the wood factory near here, and you can see I've gained permission from the SS boss to come and find you."

I looked up at him, marvelling at his ability to inspire such confidence. He was quite remarkable. He had managed to engineer the situation to our advantage. I adored him and idolized him.

"I'll come again," he promised. "Now I have to go to the kitchen and speak to one of the cooks." He held my face in his hands for a moment and then kissed me tenderly on the cheek. "I am going to arrange for her to let you have a little extra food here and there," he said, then he turned me around and nudged me gently towards the barrack door and was gone.

I walked back to my place on the bench in a dream. It was the first time I had seen him since "Canada."

Everyone had stopped work and was looking at me with awe. I felt radiant and must have shone with happiness because all the other women were smiling back at me. They were genuinely glad that something good could happen even in that terrible place.

I had absolute faith in Pappy. I was convinced that at last everything would start to improve and that he would be able to arrange for me to have some extra potatoes, anything to relieve the hollow feeling of intense hunger that gnawed at my insides all day and night.

That evening after work, I walked tentatively towards the kitchen barrack. As I showed my face at the door a friendly, buxom Polish girl spotted me.

"What a man your father is!" she said smugly, clucking her tongue and rolling her eyes to the ceiling. "And he has arranged this for you."

She handed me a bowl of warm vegetables which I grabbed and devoured on the spot, while she stood smiling at me. It was heaven.

Every evening after that I went to the kitchen door for some delicious scraps. But the most satisfying dish of all was a steaming bowl of salty left-over potato water. It was the best thing I had ever tasted. How stupid we had been in the past, I thought, to have thrown this nourishing and delicious meal straight down the drain!

I was so proud of Pappy. Even in prison uniform with his shaven head, my father still radiated a charm that women found quite irresistible. Even to see a male prisoner was an experience for any woman in the camp, so the story got around that my father and I were somehow protected by the SS. It was not true, of course, but this reputation ensured that from that time onwards the Kappos treated me with a certain amount of respect and refrained from bullying me.

Each time an SS woman or Kappo came round to inspect my work, she would stop and say, half-sarcastically, "And how is your father?"

At the end of October, I was called out again. There was Pappy once more, assuring me that Heinz was alright, and that news was coming in of the Allied offensive.

"Evertje, I'm convinced the war cannot last much longer," he said. "Have hope — it will soon be all over."

We exchanged looks of such yearning and love that I still see his face like this in my dreams.

November 1944

The chill of the Polish autumn replaced the long hot summer, and then the cold of winter began to creep up on us. Appel was still called twice a day, at dawn and in the evening. As the north winds blew across the plains, the SS guards clothed themselves with thick overcoats, the Kappos wrapped themselves up with extra layers of clothing, but we were given nothing more. The issue was still just a pair of knickers and one overgarment, and the shuffling shoes that made us look even more feeble than we already were. We shivered to stay alive.

Although the barracks where I worked at my plaits was an enclosed wooden hut, there was no flooring, just bare earth through which seeped the damp and cold. We sat all day working at trestle tables with our feet on the icy ground. Sometimes I put a piece of cloth under my numbed feet, but if a Kappo noticed, I would be forced to pick it up. I longed for a pair of snug, warm socks.

I started to develop frostbite in my toes. During the night when the warmth from my sleeping companions began to thaw my icy feet the excruciating pain would wake me up. I would lie there sobbing, praying for Pappy to come again and save me. Each day the cold in the work barracks and the sleeping quarters became more unbearable. But Pappy did not come.

By now my toes had large septic holes in them, so that I could hardly walk. During the nights, as the blood returned to my feet, I lay moaning in agony. Franzi kept repeating, "You must go to the hospital."

I was too frightened to agree. Selections were being held all the time. Though they were losing the war, the Nazis were pressing on with their meticulously planned annihilation of the Jewish people. The inhuman regime of the SS, the lack of hygiene and the intense cold hastened our deaths. Once people went into hospital, most of them were never seen again.

"I don't want to go to hospital," I said stubbornly. "I know I'll be kept there and then selected."

After work that same evening, when forty or so of us were due for our weekly shower, we were told that the usual showers were out of order, and we would have to use others in a different camp. We were horrified; we were sure that it was a ruse to get us into the gas chambers.

As we were marched along, we believed that these were our last moments on earth. We all stayed very close together. Franzi held my hand for comfort. We entered the ante-chamber to the showers without saying a word. When the command came to take our clothes off, we all stood absolutely still and made no attempt to undress. The entire group of women refused to cooperate. None of us was going to walk willingly into a gas chamber.

The Kappos started to yell at us.

"Filthy Jew pigs — get yourselves ready."

But this time, since we were convinced that we were being ordered to get ready to die, none of us moved an inch. No matter how much the Kappos screamed at us or beat us with their truncheons, we remained passive and uncooperative.

The Kappos were completely nonplussed. This was the first group resistance they had encountered from us, and they did not know how to handle it.

"These are showers, you fools," they shouted. "You will be shot if you don't go in."

Still we did not move. It was a moment of defiance. Although I did not feel very brave, I said to myself, *When I die, Mutti and I will be together again.*

Eventually they called for reinforcements. The building was surrounded by dozens of armed Germans with Alsatian dogs. Several soldiers stepped inside and pointed rifles at us, but still we stood quietly, resisting our fate.

An officer strode in, quickly took in the situation and called out in polite German, "I can assure you that you have nothing to fear. If one of you will inspect the showers, you will see that we mean you no harm."

This time it was true! They opened the doors and we could see hot water raining down. We cried and laughed with relief, but we also felt a little proud of ourselves. We had stood up to their threats with a courage that had surprised us all.

After the shower we were at last issued with warmer clothes. I was handed some knickers, two odd shoes and a heavy man's overcoat which was so long and cumbersome that I could hardly walk in it, but it was a shelter around my naked body and kept me a little warmer that night.

It must have been about noon the next day when a new group of women arrived at our workhuts. I recognized some of them because they were Dutch and had been in our transport train from Westerbork to Auschwitz. We had suffered our quarantine weeks together.

Suddenly one of them saw me sitting there and called to the others. They rushed over to me and all began speaking at once.

"Eva! Thank God you are alive!"

"We have something to tell you!"

"We have some wonderful news for you!"

"We have been staying in the hospital block . . ." I was so confused; everyone was talking to me at the same time, but I understood just one thing.

Mutti was alive! She was lying in the hospital, breathing and alive. Minni had saved her.

13

Mutti's Story

[Eva's mother takes up the story]

Early October 1944

My last glimpse of Eva as I was taken away with the other women who had been selected, was of her standing there naked, in tears, with Franzi's arms around her. As armed guards led us away, I felt that I had just forsaken my daughter at the moment when she needed me most. I had never ever felt so desperate.

We were taken to a barrack in the middle of a walled courtyard. I knew that the building had been used to house prisoners suffering from "Chris," a highly infectious skin disease. I also realized that it was now used to house those prisoners who had been selected to be gassed. The guards slammed and locked the doors behind them as they left.

We were now in the hands of several young Kappos who handed us blankets to cover our naked, shivering bodies. Nobody spoke, and though I sensed the pity that the girls felt for us, we all knew it was no use consoling one another. There must have been about thirty of us locked in together. We were given nothing to eat or drink. The only amenities were the two buckets at each end of the barrack.

We were completely exhausted and fell down on the straw palliasses which were shared by all of us. Throughout that night I slept fitfully, thinking about my life up to this point and longing to be together with Erich and my children. I wished so desperately that they could live to enjoy all that life had to offer, and that Eva could be allowed to experience the joys of love and motherhood. If I thought that when I died my strength could go into her, it would be easier to accept my death.

Dear God, I prayed, *give her that chance.*

DURING THE NIGHT some women sobbed quietly; others screamed hysterically for hours, going completely out of their minds, banging their fists against the doors until they collapsed from exhaustion. We had no water, no food, no clothes, nothing. I thought that they must have completely forgotten us. We had been locked in to die slowly and some women lay stiff on their bunks, as if they were dead already.

The next morning a Kappo appeared and told us that we could go out into the courtyard if we wanted, but most of the women preferred to remain inside.

I recognized a woman from the Dutch group who, I knew, was very religious. She tried to assemble some of the unhappy creatures around her to pray, but only a few joined her. I went outside into the courtyard and heard voices and marching from the other side of the wall, but it seemed to me that those noises were part of another world. When I returned inside, I tried to talk to some of the women, but none responded. The hours went by very slowly, and when it got dark, we tried to sleep again, to forget our thirst and hunger and misery. During the night we were joined by approximately a hundred more women who were destined to share our fate.

Around noon of the second day, the doors were unlocked and we were assembled in the courtyard, where we were offered some watery soup.

Why are they doing this? I remember thinking. *We're all about to die. Why bother to feed us?*

It occurred to some of the women that the soup might be poisoned, so they started to cry.

"Well, I'll have some anyway," I said loudly. "What difference will it make?" And I stepped forward for my share.

Others started to follow my example and stood in line for the soup. There did not seem to be anything wrong with it, and we drank thirstily, passing the mugs from hand to hand.

Immediately after the soup, clothes were brought in and distributed. Nobody cared what they put on, and I found a dark flannel dress with white dots which was very wide and hung down to my feet.

Appel was ordered and we waited to be counted. Some women were so weak that they fell to their knees while a Kappo screamed at them to get up. We waited silently, some barely breathing.

Eventually, two SS officers walked briskly into the courtyard and spoke to the Kappo. One took a small piece of paper from his top pocket and handed it to her. The Kappo walked along the lines of emaciated, lice-infected women, calling out two numbers from the paper. To my astonishment I realized that one was mine. I stepped forward and held out my tattooed arm. So did another woman.

"You two come along with us to Dr. Mengele," said one of the SS men.

Mengele's reputation was well-known in the camp. The Kappos, eager to spare no one's feelings, had reported to us every evil thing that he did. They told us these things mainly to terrify and intimidate us, but also, I suspected, to relieve themselves of their own feelings of complicity and guilt.

I knew Mengele conducted gruesome experiments on females without anaesthetics and that he had a particular interest in using twins in his pseudo-scientific research.

"If you're a twin, watch out, Mengele will be after you!" the Kappos had sneered, adding, "It is *they* who are doing this to you, not us. We only obey orders."

I was quite bewildered. *I'm not a twin,* I thought. *Why would he want me?*

The Kappo roughly pushed me and the other prisoner forward, and we were marched out by the SS to a nearby building. I was immediately escorted into a room where I recognized Dr. Mengele sitting at a desk. He glanced up at me.

"You. Undress!" he ordered.

I slipped off my dress obediently and stood naked before him.

He got up and spent some time scrutinizing my body, walking slowly around me and eyeing me from all sides.

"You have family in this camp?" he said slowly.

"Yes, my husband and my children," I replied.

"Nobody else?" he prompted me.

I suddenly realized that it must have been at Minni's intervention that I had been called out and he was referring to her.

"Oh yes! My cousin Minni is here too," I exclaimed.

He nodded. "Get dressed," he said crisply and ordered me outside.

I waited in disbelief until the other prisoner — a little, thin woman about my age who later told me she was French — came out. Together we were taken, stumbling, towards another barrack and delivered to the Kappo in charge.

The Kappo handed us bread and black substitute coffee,

after which the two of us were allowed to lie down on a bunk, which was empty as all the women had gone out to work. My companion, Loretta, and I clung to each other, talking over our luck and wondering what was next for us. My hope was that Minni would come to take me to the hospital.

But that same evening, during Appel, the Kappo from the Death Block appeared, shouting out that she was two short for her "consignment." Perhaps because I was a few inches taller than the others the Kappo spotted me.

"You!" the Kappo came over and poked me with her finger. "You big horse! Come, and that one next to you," she said. "I will take you both!"

I could not believe it. I had just been spared and now, once more, I was being sentenced to death. It was the worst kind of cruelty.

Loretta and I were soon imprisoned in the Death Block again. We lay together in a corner, waiting with the other doomed women who had been starved and weakened into submission.

At about midnight we heard lorries pulling up outside. Then the sound of boots and dogs barking.

"*Sau Juden* — get up and move out!" the Kappos ordered, and we all knew that this was the end for us.

The doors were flung open and several young soldiers, some with rifles pointed at us, formed a passageway to the tail end of the lorries.

When we emerged from the barrack, I was struck by the brilliance of the full moon. It shone down out of a vast empty sky and bathed our pale flesh in a pure white light. The beauty of the night was in stark contrast to the ugly scene ahead of me. I was in a line moving silently and without protest towards a female SS officer who sat at a small table with a list in front of her. As each woman stepped up to the table, the SS woman checked the number of her tattoo against the list. Behind her, lorries waited to take us to the gas chambers. First, however, it was necessary to check that the cargo was correct. In the allocation of death, as in all things, the Germans were very precise.

Resigned to their fate, the line of women moved with dignity towards the lorries until suddenly one prisoner called out feebly, "*Frau Obersturmführerin,* I am the daughter of a German officer who fell in the First World War."

The officer shrugged.

"I am only sixteen," pleaded another girl. "Please spare me. Please let me live."

But there was no emotion on the face of the officer, who continued to check her lists.

This is really the end for me, I thought, *and Minni won't even know what happened. No one can save me now!*

In front of me was Loretta, and as she came to the table she said boldly, "*Frau Obersturmführerin,* we two do not belong here. They have taken us from another block."

"Is that so?" the officer looked up. "What are your numbers?"

"A/6893."

"And I am A/5271," I said.

"Indeed?" The pencil was moving down the paper. I felt sick with apprehension as numbers were checked. The officer frowned and turned on the Kappo.

"Have these two women been brought here separately?" She was furious at the contravention of orders.

The Kappo started to whine, "I had to make up my numbers. I had to have a full consignment."

The SS woman sprang up and grabbed hold of her, hitting her so violently that she fell grovelling onto the ground. Then, as Loretta and I looked on, the lorry doors were slammed and the driver was ordered to pull away. As the lorry drove off, we were taken to another barrack.

During the night the crematorium burned for many hours, and flames shot from the chimneys high into the clear dark sky.

*Me as a baby with Mutti
and my brother Heinz
in Vienna in 1930.*

Pappy at the age of twenty.

*The house in Vienna
where we lived until 1935.*

*Pappy and Mutti shortly
after they met in 1920. My father
is eighteen, my mother fifteen.*

Heinz, Mutti and me in Tyrolean costume in the Tyrol in 1935.

With Heinz and Mutti by an Austrian lake in 1933.

On the beach in Belgium in 1939: (left) Pappy and Mutti, (right) Heinz, Mutti and me, (below) me, Heinz and a refugee friend.

Jacky and me in Brussels, dressed up as a prince and princess.

In Brussels in 1939:
Kitty (another
refugee friend)
Heinz, Jacky
and me.

In the garden of
the boardinghouse
in Brussels:
(center left)
by myself, (right)
with Heinz.

Heinz and me in Brussels.

*Heinz playing his guitar
outside our apartment
in 1941.*

*A school
photo of me
in 1940.*

*The Merwedeplein,
Amsterdam. We lived on the
left side. The Franks lived
on the right.*

*Heinz, Mutti
and me in
Amsterdam
in the
summer of
1940.*

On my bicycle on the Merwedeplein with my friend Jenny in 1941.

Pappy's passport. In 1940 my father's passport had to be exchanged for a German one. Jewish males had the name "Israel" added to their first name, all females the name "Sara."

A portrait of Mutti painted by Pappy while in hiding.

One of many paintings made in hiding by Heinz. It shows Heinz himself studying in an imaginary room. Pappy hid all the paintings under the floorboards of their room and, after the war, Mutti and I were able to retreive them.

A still life I painted under the guidance of Mrs. Reitsma in 1948.

My friend Franzi (with suitcase in hand), whom I first met in a Dutch prison and who was my companion in Birkenau. This picture was taken in 1942 with her brother (left) and sister (center right), both of whom died in the camps, a friend (right) — Herman Pos, who later became a renowned violinist — and her two nieces who survived

With Mrs. De Bruin on a visit to Pappy and Heinz in 1943.

The railway line into Birkenau.

On the ramp: (left) on arrival men and women were separated and (right) then divided into two columns, one destined for the camp, the other for the gas chambers.

An aerial view of a section of the camp.

Inside a barrack in Birkenau.

A heap of spectacles in the sorting camp known as "Canada" where I worked in the summer of 1944.

The electrified wire at Auschwitz.

One of the gates to the main Auschwitz camp.

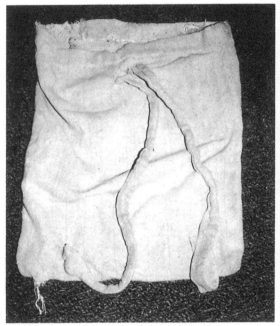

The rucksack sewn by Mutti for carrying our few belongings from Russia back to Amsterdam.

The Russian army blouse issued to us in Odessa by the Red Army.

This is me trying it on in 1988.

Franzi after the war in 1950.

Minni — I took this photo of her when she visited us in Holland in 1950.

On the Prinsengracht in 1950 during my lunch break from the photographic studio nearby where I worked.

My wedding in Amsterdam in 1952: (left to right) Mutti, Otto Frank, me, my husband Zvi, Zvi's mother and my grandmother, Helen.

With Zvi in our first home in Cricklewood, northwest London, in 1954.

In 1962 on the terrace of the Franks' house in Basel where Mutti still lives — Mutti, grandmother and I with my three daughters, baby Sylvia, Jacky (center) and Caroline.

The wedding of Mutti and Otto in Amsterdam in 1953.

Mutti and Otto in 1961.

On the beach in Cornwall: Caroline, Jacky, Otto, Mutti and Sylvia.

Mutti and Minni (left) in Israel in 1970.

The memorial for members of the Jewish Liberal congregation of Amsterdam who were victims of the Holocaust. The memorial is in the Jewish cemetery outside the city. The names are inscribed on both sides.

A detail of the memorial showing the names of Pappy and Heinz and the Frank family.

Mutti and me in 1986 holding a photo of Anne Frank.

14

Mutti

[Eva's story continued]

I was overwhelmed when I heard that Mutti was still alive. For the past two months I had believed she had been gassed. I burst into tears. Franzi ran over and put her arms round me and everyone in the workhut was looking at me — even the Kappos were smiling. It was the only day that I did not achieve my quota of plaits, but no one told me off.

For the next week I waited outside whenever I could, hoping to see Pappy and tell him the news. He had promised to come back soon, and I knew that he would. I longed to see the happiness on his face as I whispered in his ear, "Mutti is alive, Mutti is safe!"

But he never came.

It began to dawn on me then that I had found my mother but lost my father.

MY FROSTBITTEN FEET were getting worse. The holes in my toes were filled with yellow pus and I could only hobble around. Franzi kept insisting that I report to hospital. I knew the risk, but now that I had heard the wonderful news that Mutti was there, I felt more inclined to go. I hoped above all that I would be able to see her. I put myself on the list for medical treatment, knowing I would have to wait at least a week before it was my turn as only ten or twelve people were seen a day. Exactly one week later, at the dawn Appel, my number was called and I joined the daily sick party and was marched to the hospital block.

I prayed I would see Minni when I arrived, and to my joy she was still assistant to the doctor in the surgery. I saw her when she came out to fetch the next patient.

"Minni!" I called to her quietly. She looked up, but she did not recognize me.

"I'm Eva!" I said.

She let out a shriek and rushed over at once to embrace me. She held me at arm's length to have a good look at me. I must have been a funny sight: my head was shaven, my cheeks were dark red from the bitter cold outside and two odd shoes poked out from beneath the man's size overcoat which hung down to my ankles.

Minni was delighted. "She's my cousin — doesn't she look well!" she informed the Jewish doctor.

She asked if she could take me to see my mother, to which he agreed.

Minni took my hand and led me through the surgery to the back of the hospital barrack. The stench — urine, stale flesh and death — hit my nostrils. I saw rows upon rows of narrow bunks, three high, with two people in every bed. Minni walked me along the rows and suddenly pointed to a top bunk. She left me there and returned to the surgery.

I stepped on to the lower bunk and pulled myself up to the level of the top one.

"Mutti, Mutti!" I called.

A pitiful figure with a shaved head jerked upright and

stared at me in disbelief. Her gaunt face mouthed "Evertje," and she grasped hold of my hand.

Very slowly and painfully she lowered herself down from the top bunk, and then we were in each other's arms once more. She was almost starved to death. Her cheeks were hollow; her blue eyes had faded and sunk into the sockets of her skull. Her arms and hands were paper-thin, and she could barely stand upright. She was like a leaf — but she was alive.

She looked me over, in wonder.

"Darling, you are still sturdy!" she whispered. "Thank God. You look like an apple with such lovely red cheeks." But when she opened my coat to have a closer look, she saw that there wasn't much left of me either.

We sat together on the edge of the lower bunk while she told me how Minni was protecting her by keeping her in the hospital. She had a continuous temperature and no strength left to work. She spent most of her time lying on the bunk. I told her all my news: where I was working, that I had seen Pappy again and he had told me Heinz was alive. It was wonderful for us to know that our family was intact in such circumstances. By the time Minni came back for me, our spirits and faith in God were restored.

The doctor looked at my feet and diagnosed advanced frostbite. He said I should be hospitalized for treatment. "But you will have to wait your turn."

On the way out Minni put her arm round my shoulder. "I promise to pull as many strings as I can to get you in here. It won't be long. Then you'll be safe here with me."

Time was an important factor. December had arrived and with it the worst blizzards and lowest temperatures of the year. At long last, the Russians had their feet in Poland and were advancing. Every day the sound of gunfire came a little closer and, between the snowstorms, German and Russian planes droned constantly overhead. The atmosphere in the camp had become very edgy, and the morale of the camp organization was deteriorating. The guards were nervous. Their behavior towards us vacillated between friendliness and anger.

Rumors now began to circulate among the inmates that the Germans had tried to hide the evidence of the death camps by bulldozing the crematoriums. It was the most tremendous relief, although we hardly dared believe it was true. Anyway, we did not delude ourselves. We knew that we were still at the mercy of the Nazis and there were many other ways they could murder us.

Starvation was taking its daily toll. Women, exhausted in body and spirit, would work through their final day, go to sleep and never wake up. This was becoming the most common form of death.

We longed for liberation, but the end of the war seemed too far off for us. Every day could have been our end. Warmth was a forgotten comfort. There were no provisions for heat or extra clothes — except those you took from the dead — and there was no food to warm you up. Even the soup was tepid by the time it was distributed. We tried to hang on but we did not dare to hope. We feared that if the Russians came too close and the Germans had enough time before retreating, they would lock us up in the barracks and burn us alive.

In the meantime the Germans had started a slow evacuation of the camp. Every few days SS men and women would walk around the barracks with Kappos, picking out those to be evacuated to other camps. We didn't know whether it was a good thing or a bad thing to leave Birkenau. Some women tried to look strong and eager so that they would be picked. Others tried to appear small and insignificant to avoid being noticed.

Now that I knew Mutti was waiting for me to join her in hospital, the last thing I wanted was to be picked out and moved on.

The depletion of our numbers began to show. Every other day another thirty or forty women were removed from our barrack to go on to transports back into the heart of Germany. Each time the choice became more limited. I kept my head down, plaiting and praying, whenever the SS came by.

Eventually they stopped behind me. "We'll have this one," said an SS officer.

"That one's a protected child," warned the Kappo. "It might be wiser to leave her alone."

"Well, leave her then," he snapped. "We'll take that one beside her instead," and pointed to Franzi. She was roughly pulled up by the Kappo and told to go outside.

Franzi shrugged and bent down to kiss me good-bye. I hugged her hard. She had been a constant companion and a dear friend. I watched helplessly as she joined the consignment to an unknown destination. We had been thrown together by an evil fate, and there was no knowing if we would ever see each other again. I felt so grateful to have known her. She had given me comfort and courage when I had been at my lowest, and now she had to go instead of me. I needed to stay behind because of Mutti.

At that moment as I sat at the bench alone with the empty chair beside me, I knew Pappy's prayers had been answered again and I felt the hand of God truly protecting me.

16 December 1944
German counter-offensive, Battle of the Bulge

At Appel in the third week of December several women were called by their numbers to stand on one side. No one knew what it was for. Each time we were separated from the main group we expected something dreadful to happen to us, to suffer some unbearable punishment for a minor wrong-doing. The last number called was mine.

I moved forward and stood in line with nine others, watching apprehensively as the rest went off to work. Then, to my joy, we were marched towards the hospital block.

I knew it was vital to contact Minni as soon as possible so that she could use her influence and reunite me with Mutti. When we arrived, we stood in a corridor waiting for a place on any bed where the second sleepmate had died. We were not allowed to move from the spot, and we waited for hours, sitting on the floor. The orderlies were walking around freely, so I finally plucked up enough courage to ask one if she could find my cousin, Minni.

"Minni?" she exclaimed. "What a wonderful woman! She was my friend in Prague and here too. I'll fetch her for you."

Minni had been expecting me for days, but she had been too busy to check that day's admittance list. Now she led me to my mother's section where she arranged for Mutti to be moved to an empty bunk and there I joined her. At last we were together again.

We lay cuddling each other for days. With the sound of intermittent gunfire and air-raid sirens as background noise, we talked in whispers day and night about everything that had happened to us in those months we had been apart, which had seemed like years of torment. As we talked, it became clear that Minni, with God's help, had saved both our lives.

15

Liberation

M utti and I lay in our hospital bunk and listened to the sound of the guns. Sometimes the cannon fire seemed very close, then it would drift away again and cease. Days darkened into nights without any change in our condition. Scraps of information no longer reached the hospital block because the working barracks had all been evacuated. Every "able-bodied" person had been force-marched out of the camp westwards. There were no new admittances or discharges. The only exits were those of the dead. Many people were dying every day of starvation, disease and hypothermia.

We sensed that the Russians were advancing. We waited for them, alternating between hope and despair. We prayed for them to arrive, but we knew nothing of their progress. Nobody seemed to know what was happening. In any event, we were very scared that we would be eliminated before they arrived. We couldn't believe the Germans would actually leave us to be liberated by the Russians.

There were fewer Germans around now, and we were left alone more often. Appels had ceased. It was Christmastime, but we were hardly aware of that. Mutti and I lay together on the bunk, huddled under thin, ragged blankets. No one really thought that there was a chance we would survive.

Minni's indomitable spirit was the one thing we were sure of. She was incredible. She held everyone together with great strength, showing undiminished cheerfulness as she organized the rations of bread and tea, and distributed the small amounts of medicine available. She spent the days constantly on the move, walking up and down the ward, directing the three other nurses in their duties of ministering to the dying and carrying out the dead. Every time she passed us she would give our bunk a determined slap and repeat, "We will get through."

We were terrified of our fate, but Minni's cheerful courage seemed to radiate hope and prevented us from giving up.

On our bunk, Mutti and I fantasized about what we would do when we were free again. We talked about warm baths with soap, sleeping between clean sheets, eating with a knife and fork — all the civilized delights that we had taken for granted and that had been denied us for what seemed like a lifetime.

Our thoughts always centered on food. We invented glorious menus containing all our favorite dishes. How we would gorge ourselves! We imagined eating boiled potatoes, spreading butter on fresh bread and crunching our teeth into firm apples. We would pretend we were in a restaurant in Amsterdam. First of all we would select our soup, then the main course (I always chose roast chicken with rice and cauliflower) and then we would lie there, dreaming of delicious desserts — pancakes filled with jam or cream, chocolate pudding, apple pie. I always wanted to end my meal with a glass of milk, for which I had a terrible craving. And all the while our stomachs ached with starvation.

AT THE BEGINNING of January the SS appeared at the door of the barrack and shouted, "Everybody who can get up and walk — come outside."

Minni rushed over to us looking very agitated.

"Get up," she said sternly. "You have to come."

"But Mutti is too weak," I said.

"She will just have to make the effort," said Minni firmly, and swept along the lines, insisting that anyone who could get out of their bunk and stand up had better do so and get outside.

Mutti's emaciated condition had left her in a desperately weak state, but she was determined to stay with me from now on.

"Of course I can get up," she whispered. She feared we would be killed if we did not get outside. Only her willpower was giving her enough strength to stand up.

As soon as she managed to put her feet on the ground, I wrapped her in a ragged blanket. I half-dragged, half-carried her out of the door. It was the first time she had been outside for months, and she was almost fainting with the effort. She was very frail but totally determined that we should stay together. She leaned against me as we stood in the last row.

It was about eleven in the morning and bitterly cold. The temperature was far below zero. The icy air hit us, freezing the moisture on our bodies and making our face muscles so stiff that they stopped working. About half the women from the hospital block had managed to drag themselves outside.

The scene took my breath away. There was a clear, blue sky with no clouds at all. Snow lay still on the ground. It had transformed the entire compound, shrouding the huts and dirt tracks with a sheet of unblemished white. The land looked like Siberia. The bare ugliness of the camp had been smoothed over and turned, magically, into a winter fairyland.

We waited, assembled in neat rows, for further instructions but nothing happened. The SS had disappeared, leaving the Kappos standing around disconsolately, not knowing what was expected of them. We could all hear guns in the distance. We stood there for two hours, shivering inside our blankets.

Suddenly there was the wailing of an air-raid siren and agitated SS men reappeared, yelling at us to get back inside.

At dusk we were ordered out again. We stood there while the sun went down and it became darker and colder. Then there was another siren, so we all crept back into our cold bunks, frozen and shivering and very grateful to get our tiny portion of bread. Everyone was very nervous and frightened — including the Germans.

Although we remained inside throughout that night, we just could not get warm again. The cold had seeped into our frail bodies, and during those hours quite a few people died. In the morning I lay and watched as the dead were hauled off their bunks and dragged out into the snow by the nurses.

I saw Minni carry out several of her friends in her arms. Her face was haggard and blank. She came over to Mutti once or twice and touched her head, pleading, "Hold on."

This harassment went on for three days. Sometimes we were called out during the night to stand for hours in the bitter cold. Each time, when we were ordered outside again, more and more people stayed inside and did not attempt to obey the commands. By the evening of the third day I, too, decided that I had had enough. I wasn't going to see Mutti subjected to any more misery.

"It will be another false alarm, anyway," I assured her. So

when the command came to get up and get outside, we stayed on our bunk and fell into an exhausted sleep.

When we awoke next morning, everything was still and quiet. There was no activity and the barrack seemed almost empty. I got up and went outside to investigate. It was a curious sensation; there was no one to be seen. Every SS guard and dog had disappeared. All the Kappos had vanished and most of the hospital patients had left too. Minni and the nursing staff had also gone.

It was another bitterly cold day but bright. Bodies of the dead lay at the side of the barrack slung one on top of the other. In the whole camp, which had housed tens of thousands, there were now only one or two hundred souls left. Eighty percent of these were too ill to move at all and lay waiting for death. The rest of us, a tiny contingent of living skin and bones, hung on with rising hope.

We knew we would have to try to survive alone until the Russians came and that might take several days or even weeks. And so we attempted to organize ourselves.

One Polish woman, Olga, who was not Jewish but had been a communist political prisoner, took command. She decided that she and I, with one or two other fitter inmates, should walk over to the kitchen block to see what food might be available. We also needed to find fresh water as all the pipes were frozen.

We wrapped ourselves in blankets and trudged across the snow to the kitchen barrack. We pushed against the doors, expecting them to be barred, but to our amazement they yielded immediately. What we saw when we entered made us cry out in delight. There, stacked up on the shelves which lined the walls, were hundreds of loaves of black bread — far more than we could ever eat in a year. It was like finding a treasure trove. We seized a loaf each and crammed chunks of bread into our mouths. We gorged ourselves on this limitless supply, then we filled our arms with as many loaves as we could carry and headed back to our barrack.

During the five-minute walk I felt a wonderful elation. I was excited beyond belief and I could not wait to distribute the food — to be able to give strength back to everyone there. As I went round the bunks, tearing off huge hunks of bread and pressing them into the skeleton hands of the bedridden inmates, I cried *Thank God* to myself over and over again. Some of them were too ill to eat much but they clasped the precious portions tightly against their bodies. We had barely taken enough, but we were too weak to go back for more.

By now I was utterly exhausted and very confused. What if the Germans returned during the night and caught us? What if the Russians did not come in time to save us? I was extremely frightened because we were so alone. I began to re-alize that we might not survive after all, simply because we could not look after ourselves. There were so few able-bodied women who had enough strength even to walk about.

It was midday when Mutti and I ate some more bread. I lay down on my bunk to regain some strength, closed my eyes with relief and drifted into a fretful sleep. I was brought back to reality by Olga shaking me vigorously.

"Get up and come down!" she ordered. "I need you."

"Not now," I protested. "Please let me rest. I am worn out."

"I need you to carry out some dead bodies," she said firmly.

It was as if an immense black cloud had descended on me.

"No! No!" I cried out in panic.

She grabbed hold of me and pulled me up off the bunk. She held me by my shoulders and turned me around to face her.

"You are young and still strong enough," she said, looking firmly at me. "There is no one else. It is your duty. If you can carry bread, then you can carry out the dead."

Through my panic and fear I could hear Mutti saying faintly, "Leave her, she's too young. I will do it."

Suddenly I came to my senses. I knew that Mutti had no strength at all. That was the moment I grew up — it was time I looked after Mutti.

IT WAS THE WORST TASK I have ever had to perform in my whole life. I carried out the dead. Some were friends with whom I had talked about our liberation. Many were so diseased and stinking that it took all my courage to touch them. It was now dark and the moon shone on the other bodies which stared at me open-eyed from stiffened mounds of dead flesh and bones. Here were faces I had come to know and respect. I looked on mouths now agape that had given me wise counsel and encouragement; eyes that had gazed on me, lovingly, remembering their own dead children. I had always tried to "stand in" for their loved ones and give back just a little of that love. There had been so little that we could give each other except love.

It was the first time I had been so involved with the dead, and it horrified me to see the waste of people cut down in the prime of their lives. None of them were older than forty; many were much younger — women who had managed to retain enough hope to survive almost until the end.

I saw more people die in the next few days than I had seen in my whole time at Birkenau.

THE SOUND OF GUNFIRE was intensifying in the distance, getting nearer all the time. I was with a sortie that went back to the kitchens the next morning for a more thorough inspection. We were beginning to feel a little bolder now and started to move more freely around the camp site.

I spotted a hole in the wire fencing between sections of the camp.

"I'm going to go through," I said, assuming the electric current had been switched off.

Luckily, I was right and soon two others followed me. Everything on the other side was quite deserted, but in there we came upon the barracks where all the provisions had been stored.

It was like the re-enactment of a story from the Brothers Grimm. The first barrack was stacked with clothing, every article of apparel you could imagine from boots to berets. The second barrack held blankets and eiderdown, all shelved neatly like a Swiss laundry house. The third barrack held the food stores.

As we entered the last barrack, we could see boxes of wrapped cheeses, jars of jam, sacks of flour, heaps of potatoes — food beyond our wildest dreams, and we starving skeletons just grabbed what we could easily lay our hands on and sat there and ate.

Eventually we returned to the second barrack and helped ourselves to large blankets to use as sacks. Just like Santa Claus, we filled our blankets with all the food we could manage. We knotted the four corners together and slung them over our shoulders. Excitedly, I set off to return to Mutti with the greatest of treasures, and as we stepped outside to carry back our plunder it started to snow again, soft white flakes falling on our heads.

It suddenly occurred to us that we could revisit the clothes store for warmer clothes. I found a splendid pair of black leather military boots, all polished and clean. I put them on my poor swollen feet. They were large men's boots with plenty of room, my first shoes without holes and protection at last from the bitter weather. I felt so smart as I plodded through the snow, keen to show them to Mutti. I did not notice any pain in my toes at all.

In the next few days we returned time and time again to find everything we needed, including all kinds of tools, hatchets, hacksaws, picks, knives. We distributed as much food and clothes as we could to the bedridden.

Mutti managed to accompany me the next day. She was eager to share my excitement, although she was still very shaky. She held on to my arm as we trudged slowly through the thick layer of snow that had fallen overnight. She was amazed at the extent of the stock. She pulled out some clothes and found a dark blue woolly dress with a high polo-neck collar. Then she chose some long grey woollen stockings and a pair of black sturdy lace-up shoes which fitted her exactly. As she stood there with warm clothes covering her skinny body at last, and with her hair growing again, she asked, "Do I look alright?"

"Mutti, you look marvelous," I replied and we wept together.

The best find of all was two feather eiderdowns with snug, downy fillings. They were fairly bulky but lightweight enough to carry around. We wrapped them round our bodies, and from then on we four became inseparable!

17 January 1945
Warsaw liberated

Water everywhere was still frozen. At first, we melted snow. We would collect it in mugs or bowls, but the amount of liquid was too small for our needs. At the entrance to the camp was a little water reservoir, more of a pond in fact, which was covered with ice and snow. Olga suggested that someone should attempt to hack into the ice to try and draw out water.

I volunteered to try. So, wearing my sturdy boots, I marched with Olga down to the pond, both of us armed with axes and buckets. We were determined to succeed. Using up a great deal of our limited energy, huffing and puffing, we managed to hack the brittle ice until it cracked and flew off in large blocks. It was a long and arduous task as the ice was over a foot thick. At last the broken ice gave way, and we found ourselves staring at clear water beneath. We whooped with joy. The hole was just large enough to immerse our buckets and, feeling like Eskimos, we drew up the precious liquid and carried it back to the barrack.

We coped for a few days in this way, raiding the stores for food and smashing the ice daily for water. There was still nowhere we could really keep warm. There was no place in the barrack where we could make a fire, cook food or heat up any water. Olga and Mutti talked it over and agreed to try and find a place outside the camp to improve our living conditions.

By now, those who could fend for themselves were doing so, and the dead had no need of us.

I had noticed an empty house near the camp walls where the SS guards had been billeted. It was a custom-made wooden house, and we thought it was bound to have some heating facilities. We decided to go and investigate. Yvette, a young French woman, heard our discussion and asked if she could come along. We still felt very insecure and agreed, since four was a safer number. Just as we were gathering ourselves up to leave, we heard someone screaming outside. The barrack door was flung open and a woman yelled, "There's a bear at the gate! A bear at the gate! Come quickly!"

Cautiously, we went outside towards the open gate and there, at the entrance, was the "bear" — a huge being, covered from head to foot in bearskin with a look of utter amazement on his face. We stood and stared at each other and then, carefully, I edged towards him with joy on my face.

Our liberator stood at the entrance to the camp, alone and strong. With outstretched arms I ran to him and hugged against him . . . and although our languages were not the same, what I said to him and what he said to me was understood by us both. The Russians had come!

Part III

JOURNEY THROUGH RUSSIA

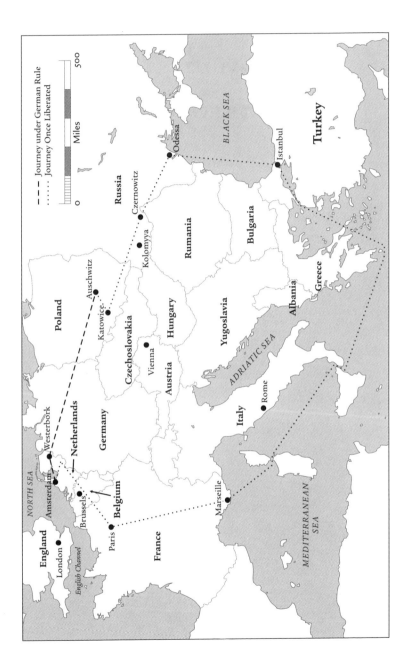

Journey under German Rule
Journey Once Liberated

Miles
0   500

NORTH SEA

England
London

English Channel

Netherlands
Westerbork
Amsterdam

Germany

Belgium
Brussels

Paris

France

Marseille

MEDITERRANEAN
SEA

Poland
Auschwitz
Katowice

Czechoslovakia
Vienna
Austria

Hungary

Italy
Rome

ADRIATIC SEA

Yugoslavia

Albania
Greece

Russia

Czernowitz
Kolomyya

Rumania

Bulgaria

Odessa

BLACK SEA

Istanbul

Turkey

16

The Russians

27 January 1945

Throughout that day our liberators entered the camp in small batches: sturdy Russian soldiers on horseback pulling armaments and provisions for the advance. They had little time to be concerned with the welfare of the inmates who remained. We hung around them, watching their every move, but the language barrier between us was too great for any real communication. We sensed they were eager to pursue the retreating Germans. They just stayed long enough to set up their field kitchen inside the compound. Soon there was the delicious aroma of hot potato and cabbage soup bubbling up from the cauldron, and we were thrilled when they beckoned us to come nearer and handed us bowls of steaming soup. I could feel the warmth penetrating my body.

Now that the Russians had arrived, our little group thought it would be quite safe to move into the quarters that had housed the SS. Late in the afternoon, we four walked through the camp gates. It was an eerie feeling. There were no guards to stop us, no dogs barking, only the sounds of horses neighing and the wind whining.

We came to the hut and tried the door. Amazingly it was not locked, and we apprehensively entered *Herr Obersturm-führerin's* living quarters. We inspected the two main rooms. They smelt clean and had the neatness of civilization about them. We all wanted to stay together for safety and companionship, so we opted for the room with four bunk beds, each with clean bedding.

More importantly there was a black iron stove in the center of the room with its supply of firewood piled high in the corner. We could hardly wait to get it going. We stoked the wood, lit it and stood around watching the flames grow. Then, sitting on the floor in our first snug accommodation, we bathed in the wonderful feeling of at last becoming warm again.

We were thoroughly sleepy by now, mentally exhausted from the tension and excitement of the day and longing to lie between clean sheets once more. The room was glowing with heat and, for the first time in many months, we took off our outside clothes and climbed on our beds. Olga chose a bottom bunk and Yvette the one above it. Mutti slid between the sheets of her bottom bunk with a look of ecstasy on her face. I threw my eiderdown on to the top, climbed up after it and snuggled down in its familiar softness. But I couldn't get to sleep for ages. I lay watching the shadows dancing on the whitewashed walls, convincing myself of what I had hardly believed possible. We had come through. We had survived.

We woke early. Outside the air was absolutely still and deadly quiet. When I looked through the window, new snow had fallen during the night.

All water facilities in the hut were frozen and we had no food with us, so we delegated Olga and Yvette to hack the ice in the pond for water while Mutti and I went to the stores. This time we discovered more underground rooms packed high with provisions. We filled two sacks with potatoes, carrots, onions and barley until we could hardly lift them and dragged them back across the snow.

Olga already had water boiling in a pan, and she soon prepared a delicious pot of thick vegetable soup. When it was ready, we guzzled it down like hungry wolves. I could not stop eating and wanted more — and then even more — but Mutti warned me not to eat so much. She was sure it would make me ill, yet I could not stop myself. Mutti was right, of course. I was sorry later when, because my body was so unused to digesting food, I found myself doubled up with stomach cramp and diarrhea. My abdomen had become terribly bloated, and I moaned with the pain of it. I implored Mutti to do something to help me out of my agony.

"Pierce a hole in my stomach to let the air out," I pleaded.

But there was not much she could do except help me over to the toilet bucket where I spent most of the night.

After that experience I was much more careful with the amount of food I ate at one time. For safety we took turns in pairs to return to the stores to collect any provisions we needed, often to the background noise of distant gunfire and the overhead droning of Russian planes.

The weather was still bitterly cold, with water frozen solid in the pipes and on the pond and between us we shared the more strenuous duty of collecting water. When it was Mutti's and my turn, we each armed ourselves with a pickaxe. The grey smoke of our breath froze on our scarves as we panted with the effort of hacking the ice away, even though it was a thinner layer that had formed over our hole during the night. It took us a good half an hour each time. We were still weak and quite exhausted and frozen by the time we drew up clean water. We only had one bucket, so we had to return several times during the day.

Olga was the strongest of us, attacking all tasks with determination. She was full of enthusiasm and energy. Being Polish she was certain she would soon be returning to her home and family. Yvette, however, was very lethargic and miserable. She suspected that no one in her family had survived. Frightened of what the future might reveal, she lay for many hours resting on her top bunk, occasionally sobbing quietly to herself.

We passed three days in this relative safety and comfort when towards night-time, after we had decided to bed down early, we heard a commotion outside and the door was suddenly kicked open. We sat up in our bunks, clutching at our covers, gasping in alarm, all our fragile sense of security immediately shattered. There in the doorway stood two strapping men dressed in long fur-lined leather coats. Great fur hats half hid their faces and their eyes glowered out from under their frost-covered eyebrows. Here were two more of our Russian bears standing transfixed at the sight of us.

After our initial fright we jumped down from our bunks and rushed over to pull them into the warmth of the room. Olga spoke to them in Polish, offering them food and trying to get information from them, but they hardly responded. They were utterly exhausted. They told her that all they wanted was sleep. We indicated they were welcome to use our beds and quickly rearranged our own sleeping places — Olga and Yvette sharing a top bunk, Mutti and I the bunk underneath. Mutti pushed me against the wall and lay protectively on the outside. Deep down we were all quite scared of these men because we had heard so many stories of Russians raping women. But we slept soundly enough through the night, and when we awoke next morning both Russians had disappeared.

We saw no more soldiers until two days later when the main vanguard of ten lorries and about a hundred men made camp near the house. The Russians were wonderful to us. They always shared their hot camp food with us while we sat around their fire exchanging stories. Contrary to the rumors, we never felt sexually threatened by them. They were honest, decent men who treated us with respect. We knew at last we were with friends.

Some could speak Polish, some German, and we heard horrific tales of what the Germans had done to their people. There was a thirteen year old in this first line whose village, including his whole family, had been wiped out. He was determined to take his revenge. Every Russian was filled with thoughts of vengeance, and they couldn't wait to lay their hands on the first Germans they came to. They vowed to terrorize all the German towns and villages they came across in return for the atrocities committed against their dear ones. It seemed to me they needed to alleviate the guilt they felt for surviving and it was a way to justify their hatred.

The first batch stayed near our camp overnight and were gone the next day. They had faced tough fighting all the way in their advance and were bound to encounter more. But they were immensely optimistic and resilient, and I grew to have nothing but love and respect for those brave Russians.

Throughout the next few days groups of advancing Russians appeared intermittently. Some were on foot, some in motorized transport, some on horseback. They camped for a day or two, shared what they had with us in the way of food and news and then moved on.

Following along behind the soldiers there were always boys trying to help in any way they could. They hung around the army, waiting for tasks, so I would wrap myself up in my quilt and go and chat with them. Some spoke broken German and somehow we managed to talk to each other. They were filled with intense and unquenched hatred for the Germans and kept repeating stories of Nazi atrocities in their home towns.

One evening, during a lull in the advance and just as we were about to go to bed, we heard a timid knock on the door. No Russians that we knew knocked timidly on doors. We didn't know what to make of it. We all crowded together and opened the door very carefully. As we peered out, we could see a tall man in his early forties dressed in striped prison uniform. He asked in a very shaky German voice if he could come inside.

He said he was an escaped prisoner and that he was starving and freezing, so we let him in. We gave him bread and soup, which he guzzled down, thanking us in polite German, which made us feel that somehow he wasn't authentic. He looked too healthy to have suffered long deprivation. We were highly suspicious of him although he was obviously terrified.

His story was that when the SS had ordered all prisoners to march away from the camp he had hidden and managed to escape the forced march. He pleaded with us to let him stay for a while, but we were all adamant that he could not. He kept asking if we had seen any Russians and which way they had gone. If he was genuine, we were sure the Russians would look after him, so deliberately we gave him wrong directions which would take him into their hands. We felt sorry for him because he was so nervous, but we were scared enough to turn him out into the night.

The next batch of Russians arrived the following morning. With them was our night intruder, who was now their prisoner. His hands were tied behind his back and he was being roughly pushed along. We were very disturbed that the Russians were treating him so harshly and told them so. We made such a great fuss about it that eventually, in exasperation, a Russian officer brought him to our door, undressed him in front of us and lifted up his arm. There underneath his armpit was a tattoo, positive proof of his SS identity. Oddly enough we weren't pleased in any way; we were extremely upset. We should have been immune to any kind of suffering, but we were not. It sickened us to imagine what was going to happen to him. It was a strange emotional reaction.

17

Outside the Gate

M y emotions, which had been numbed for so long now, began to surge back. The slightest incident made me laugh hysterically or cry uncontrollably. We still lived in apprehension as to what was to happen to us, but not with the fear of imminent death.

We now had adequate food for our needs, consisting mainly of black bread and potatoes, with vegetables like onions, carrots and swedes. We added dried lentils to thicken the soups. We supplemented our diet with cheese and condensed milk and used oil, butter and flour for cooking, but we had no fresh meat. The steaming stews the Russians shared with us had given us a taste for it.

When a new contingent of the advance arrived, we would stroll around, hoping for a helping which the Russians always gave us, but this particular morning we were unlucky. They were only moving through with horses carrying provisions for the front line. Olga and Mutti went back in to prepare food, but I stayed out to watch their preparations.

One mare seemed to be deadly tired under her burden. She lay down on the ground snorting, and no matter how the men tried to get her up, she refused to move. I watched the soldiers stand around considering what to do with her until one Russian took out his pistol and shot her through the head. They left her lying dead in the snow as they moved off. I knew it was only a horse but I was upset by the killing.

The following morning I took Olga out to show her the corpse. The stiff carcass was shrouded with newly fallen snow.

"This will mean meat stew tonight and a good stock of meat!" said Olga, being practical and not a bit squeamish.

She headed for the hut and returned with a large sharp kitchen knife. I had to keep a short distance away. I could barely watch as she bent over the corpse and cut into the soft part of the belly which looked as if it would have some good meat for stews.

Suddenly she straightened up.

"Come and take a look, Eva!" she called and, despite myself, I went over to see what she wanted to show me.

Instead of edible flesh, she had exposed a perfectly formed baby foal lying dead in its mother's womb. I was so shocked that I took one look at it and ran away. I leaned against the back of the house crying bitterly for a long time because, like everything else in Birkenau, it was dead for no good reason. I knew it was irrational. I had seen so many people die and had stood by as helplessly as I had with the foal. But when Mutti came to find me, I sobbed on her shoulder over that tiny being more than I had over anything else.

Later, however, when Olga served up a sizzling joint of horsemeat, I could not resist eating it with the others.

AFTER THAT INCIDENT there seemed to be a lull in the fighting. No more Russians appeared, and three or four days went by without the sounds of guns.

We still took turns to draw water through our hole in the little reservoir pond set about fifty meters from the house. Because we were much more relaxed now, we would go out on our own and this morning it was Mutti's turn. I watched her idly from the window as she tramped through the snow, armed with the bucket and axe. She hacked away until I saw her kneel down to draw up the water.

Just then, to my horror, two full lorry loads of German Wehrmacht screeched to a halt at the gate of the camp. Then the first lorry went on to career straight through the camp towards the hospital block. The other lorry drove towards where Mutti was standing, frozen with shock. A soldier jumped down pointing his gun at her and ordered her to get in the back. By this time the three of us were crouching down out of sight, and we could hear German voices shouting across the wasteland to the sick hospital inmates.

"Everybody out! All out! Get ready to march!"

I watched from behind the window as the terrible transport crept out of the camp with one lorry at the front and one at the back. Several soldiers walked alongside with guns pointed at the line of shuffling women. I spotted Mutti in her blue dress glancing towards the window, her face etched in terror. The line of human wretchedness slowly passed by, and we heard the droning of the lorries in low gear as they moved away into the distance until there was silence.

We had no idea whether the Germans had left any soldiers behind to set fire to the buildings to destroy evidence of the camps, but I was frantic. I could hardly believe that Mutti was going to be killed now after all we had gone through. I crouched, stunned, my fist stuffed inside my mouth trying to stifle hysterical screams.

"Try to be brave, Eva," Olga said, crawling towards me.

"God will take care of her." She tried to put her arms round me, but I pushed her away in panic.

"Keep quiet," Yvette hissed. "You'll give us all away!"

We stayed hiding on the floor for what seemed like hours. I sat hunched in a corner in deep despair, not knowing what to do. Occasionally we heard the crack of shots echoing over the still snow, but apart from that everything was quiet. By the time dusk had come, snow was again falling heavily. We assumed by now that no German soldiers had stayed behind.

Suddenly a loud knock at the door made us jump out of our skins. And then, amazingly, miraculously, we heard Mutti's voice calling, "Evertje — it's me, I'm here!"

I threw open the door and we fell into each other's arms. Tears of relief flooded down my face. My darling Mutti was safely back.

LATER, WHILE WE SAT around the stove drinking hot soup, she told us what had happened. Soon after passing through the gates of the camp so many women had collapsed that the Germans either shot them or left them to die. Mutti knew that she had to feign death. She began to drag herself more slowly through the thick snow and then collapsed to the ground, trusting to God that they wouldn't bother to waste a bullet on her. She lay there motionless as the others shambled past her. She could feel the ground tremble as the lorry wheels rolled by less than a meter away. She remained like that until she was sure it was safe to move and then made her way back to our hut in the dark.

We slept together in the same bunk that night, clasped in each other's arms once more.

The following morning when it was light we walked to-gether up the main road outside the camp to see if anyone was still alive. All was deadly silent. As far as our eyes could see, the road was strewn with the frozen bodies. Many were lying in pools of blood that stained the snow. More than a hundred women had perished in the night.

18

The Road to Auschwitz

To our relief, Russians were now reappearing in waves every two or three days, camping for a night or two then moving on. Half of them were on horseback. They always set up a bivouac with a kitchen unit, about twenty or thirty men at a time.

The four of us were very nervous and we discussed what to do. We felt we ought to find out if there were still men alive in the main Auschwitz camp. Perhaps it would be safer if we could unite with them.

It seemed that the Germans had definitely retreated, so we agreed that Yvette and I would walk to the main Auschwitz camp next day to investigate what was left there.

We wrapped up warmly, me in my quilt over my jacket, breeches and boots, and Yvette wearing a padded Russian jacket that a soldier had given her.

We set out at around eleven when the weather was best, walking side by side along the snow-covered road, following the ridges of lorry wheels. We met no one. Gusts of wind blew snow flurries into our faces as we trudged through crisp snow. The air held no noise other than the crunch of our boots. We spoke little to each other, needing all our breath and effort to walk in the bitter cold. Besides, we were both afraid of what we might encounter.

At last, after two hours or so, we saw two-storey buildings rising in the distance. These indicated the beginning of the outskirts of Auschwitz. There were now several Russian lorries parked along the road. Burly fur-clad, fur-capped Russians were around them busily repairing engines or cleaning guns. As we approached, the men turned to watch as we walked towards them, but no one said anything and no one stopped us.

By the time we found ourselves nearing the main Auschwitz camp, there was an air of activity, organization and permanence about the Russian presence. Ironically, above the gates a wrought-iron message spelt out ARBEIT MACHT FREI ("Work brings freedom"). The thought that I was free was so overwhelming that I could hardly take it in.

Russians had set up their headquarters and field kitchens and the military appeared to be in complete control. It was what we had longed for: the signs of life. We almost ran the last hundred meters, we were so excited and delighted to see men who could protect us.

As we drew nearer, other men in striped prison uniforms and berets walked slowly towards us. They were emaciated and unsteady. I searched their faces, longing to recognize Pappy or Heinz.

We made for the first brick barracks that we saw and climbed up the stairs into a long room. Inside were rows of single bunks, three high, filled with male prisoners. Some were lying down, some sat on the lower bunks. When they saw us, many got up and shuffled over to question us eagerly. We confirmed that we had walked from Birkenau and with that news they were completely overwhelmed. It was as if an electric switch had been turned on. Everyone started speaking or calling out to us at the same time. *Who were we? Were there other women alive? Had we known so and so? Were many left alive in Birkenau?*

Voices came at us from all sides in German, French, Yiddish, Polish, Hungarian, Dutch. We stood in bewilderment not knowing what to say. We were the first women they had seen since liberation, and they were anxious to know if their dear ones had survived. We could not help them because we realized that in all probability they had not.

I searched the faces for Pappy or Heinz. They were not there but I saw one face that looked vaguely familiar. He was middle-aged with hardly any face left at all, just a skeleton's skull out of which stared pale brown enquiring eyes.

"I know you," I said in Dutch, almost sure in the back of my mind that I had seen him before. He stood up slowly and painfully, tall and dignified still and bowed slightly to me.

"I am Otto Frank," he said, smiling weakly. "And you are Eva Geiringer, aren't you? The little friend of Anne." And with that he took me in his arms and hugged me.

"Is Anne with you? Have you seen her or Margot?" he asked eagerly, but I had to tell him I had not seen any of my friends from Merwedeplein in the camp.

He couldn't give me information about Pappy or Heinz either but said all able-bodied prisoners had been marched away. I sat on his bunk for a while and told him all the news that I could, and he thought it was a good idea that we move into Auschwitz where the Russians had permanent headquarters and were going to look after the prisoners. I promised to come back and see him.

The Russians filled Yvette and me with hot soup, after which I said we should get back to Mutti and Olga. Yvette was so excited to be in the company of men once more that she didn't see any point in going back and refused to accompany me. So I had to face the return walk alone.

I started along the road to Birkenau at about four in the afternoon when twilight was already falling. I was nervous at the thought of walking by myself, but there was no help for it. I trudged on for a good hour, by which time it was quite dark. There was no moon, but the sky was clear with a myriad of stars.

Suddenly, tracer bullets cracked and whizzed past my head, glowing greenish-blue in the dark. I threw myself into the snow to avoid the crossfire. All became quiet again. In the distance I heard a lorry coming but I didn't know whether it was German or Russian, so I scrambled and hid behind a bush until it had passed. Just as I was about to trudge on again, several more lorries rumbled passed me, so I remained hidden.

By this time it was extremely dark and bitterly cold. I knew if I lost my way I would not survive the night. *What if I freeze to death here and never see Mutti again?* I thought. *What will Mutti do if I don't get back tonight?*

So, calling up all my courage and energy, I came out from the bushes and tramped onwards. I whistled softly to myself for company. After a while, when I became tired of whistling, I put the corner of my eiderdown into my mouth and sucked it for comfort. I knew that corpses lay along the route. As I passed them, I could truly feel their spirits helping me on, and all of a sudden I wasn't afraid anymore. I marched steadily on until I saw the dim outline of our shelter.

Only a few weeks before I would have had fearful feelings about a house where SS officers had lived, but now as I knocked loudly on the door, I knew I had come home to Mutti.

The next morning we would leave to join the men in Auschwitz and begin to look forward to a future once more. So few women had been able to walk freely out of Birkenau, but I realized with an immense rush of gratitude and humility that I was one of them.

19

Auschwitz

February 1945

The morning was crisp and clear when we left Birkenau. A few days earlier Mutti and I had raided the stores to find a small suitcase which we filled with a change of underwear, some woollen stockings, jumpers and two dresses (skirts were useless since we had no waists). We also packed a loaf of bread. We told Olga we were determined to leave as quickly as possible. A strange Fate had made us dependent on each other, and now she joined us readily.

At first our elation carried us along — we were free and it seemed almost inconceivable that only a few kilometers behind us millions of our people had been systematically put to death.

It had snowed hard in the night, and as we three tramped through the soft, crunchy layer we could see the mounds of snow which covered the bodies from that last fateful forced-march, lining the roadway. Everything was now white and peaceful.

Our precious quilts were rolled up under our arms. Mutti and I took turns with the suitcase, but after a while it became heavier by the step. Every footprint was evidence of our determination to reach Auschwitz. Our breath vaporized in the bitter cold and we walked wearily, too anxious about what the future held in store to speak. I stumbled along with half-closed eyes, longing to see Pappy and Heinz again and imagining Pappy's face when he saw Mutti alive before him, not dead as he'd thought. He wouldn't be able to believe that among all the victims we two had survived and come back. The anticipation of our reunion gave us strength to continue.

It took more than two hours before the red-brick buildings of Auschwitz appeared on the horizon. The Russians were still around, busily organizing their provisions and troops. When we reached the first batch of soldiers, Olga walked over to them, turned to us and waved us to go on. We trudged past her and never saw her again.

I LED MUTTI to the first building I had visited before. The three-tiered lines of bunk beds were still filled with shrivelled, emaciated men, mainly young men who now looked ancient, whose grey, shaven skulls and prominent jawbones held skin without flesh beneath. Everyone looked like a living skeleton. We started to walk slowly along the rows searching for Pappy or Heinz. Eager eyes sought us out and followed us as they looked for some recognition of their own loved ones. I did not find Mr. Frank again, but we came across one man that we had known in Amsterdam and seen in Westerbork. Something about his features made Mutti stop by his bunkside.

"Mr. Hirsch?" she asked unsurely.

He lay motionless, his eyes turned towards us but without any expression.

"Mr. Hirsch," Mutti repeated, ". . . don't you know me . . . Fritzi Geiringer?"

Very gradually his expression altered, his face cleared into a weak smile and he feebly held out his hand to clutch at hers.

"I'm so pleased you're still alive," said Mutti.

"Fritzi? You've come through!" he whispered hoarsely. That's wonderful! But I can't get up to greet you," he apologized. "My leg's broken and it's tied to a plank."

We asked about Pappy and Heinz. And then he gave us the news we had dreaded to hear.

"They've gone." He shook his head at the despairing look on our faces. "They left with one of the last forced marches. Erich said anyone left behind would surely be killed by the retreating SS, so he felt he and Heinz should make the effort to go. I had no choice. I can't walk," he shrugged.

It was devastating news. We could hardly bear to look at each other we were so demoralized. Mutti patted his hand and promised to return after we had organized shelter for the night. Our hearts were heavy as we went outside. Somehow we had to go on existing. We comforted each other with the thought that Pappy and Heinz were probably in fairly good condition and that they should survive the march. We would just have to wait a little longer to be reunited.

On the top floor of the same building were small rooms occupied now by Russians and some fitter-looking inmates. We found an empty room equipped with two single wooden beds, straw mattresses, a small table and one wooden chair. Best of all, there was a door that we could close for privacy. We claimed it as our quarters and dumped our meager possessions on the beds before going down to investigate. The spoils of war were everywhere, dozens of people were wandering around plundering the stores and abandoning goods they did not want. We found washrooms on the ground floor with running cold water, but the lavatories were all blocked. We took a bucket from the corridor to use in our room as a toilet and some plates and cutlery from an abandoned pile outside. And then I came across the greatest find of all: a huge liver sausage which lay in the road ready to be grabbed. Our mouths watered at the thought of our first liverwurst sandwich for years. We would share some with Mr. Hirsch, and the idea of it totally preoccupied us until we arrived back at our room. As we pushed open the door, our hearts sank. The suitcase and all our belongings had gone! Only the quilts were left.

We sat on our beds disconsolately looking at our sausage, and, bread or no bread, I sank my teeth into it. Mutti bit some off as well, warning me again not to eat too much in one go, but I was like a starved, crazed animal and nothing in the world could stop me. The impulse to eat was so strong that I ate ravenously until there was nothing left.

It had been an emotional and tiring day. As evening drew in, we lay down on separate beds under our quilts, but my exhaustion was not strong enough to overcome my need for Mutti's warmth and after a few minutes I crept over to her bed to snuggle down beside her.

Later I woke with terrific stomach cramp that made me rush to the bucket, and there I had to spend the rest of the night, paying for my gluttony!

Next morning we went out to talk to the Russians. There seemed to be a small permanent band of soldiers who were coping with the problems of the abandoned concentration camp. Some were digging holes for latrines for the inmates; others were organizing able-bodied people to help peel the vast mounds of potatoes to be tipped into heavy black cauldrons for potato and cabbage soup. It was the mainstay food for all, troops included. Large chunks of rough, coarse maize

Tymczasowa Rada Miejska
m. Oświęcimia

L.p. 188

Zaświadcza

że Pan *Geiringer Elfriede*

urodz. dnia *13.2.1905* w *Weenen*

tatuowany numerem *A.5271* przebywał w Obozie Koncentracyjnym w Owięcimiu i obecnie udaje się do *Throhowa*

Uprasza się wszystkie Władze o udzielenie wymienionemu wszelkiej możliwej pomocy.

Oświęcim, dnia *14.2* 1945 r.

Tymczasowa Rada Miejska
m. Oświęcimia

L.p. 189

Zaświadcza

że Pan *Geiringer Eva*

urodz. dnia *14.5.1929* w *Weenen*

tatuowany numerem *A.5272* przebywał w Obozie Koncentracyjnym w Owięcimiu i obecnie udaje się do *Throhowa*

Uprasza się wszystkie Władze o udzielenie wymienionemu wszelkiej możliwej pomocy.

Oświęcim, dnia *14.2* 1945 r.

The passes issued to Mutti and me by the Russians
in Auschwitz after the liberation of the camp

bread were distributed, and there was now sufficient food to halt the symptoms of starvation. We were willing to undertake any task for extra food. A Russian officer asked Mutti to clean his office windows, which were thick with the grime of winter. There was no water but he showed us how to do it with balls of newspaper. Afterwards he gave us bread and cheese and we were very grateful.

Three young, sturdy Russian soldiers appeared early one morning armed with handsaws and muscle power and began to saw off the top two tiers of the bunks. Converting the three-tier system to something like a hospital ward allowed us to distance ourselves from the feeling of being prisoners. It comforted us to know that somebody was aware of our plight, and it was a very important step for our morale. Later we saw the wood being slung onto the fires of the field kitchen and realized it had been cut down for fuel.

There were several other Dutch women in the camp, and within the week Mutti and I had met them. Some had been captured in September and were not in such a bad state as the long-standing inmates. One of them, Rootje, was lively and friendly and of about Mutti's age. The SS had discovered her hiding place, and she'd been caught with her husband and sixteen-year-old daughter Judy. Judy had been transported to another work camp, and she envied Mutti having me with her. They soon became good friends. She was searching for her husband, but he, too, had left on one of the last marches. Rootje also spoke of Otto Frank's family, who had been in Rootje's barrack. She told us that Margot and Anne had been sent away in October and Edith had become mentally troubled, imagining they were still with her and keeping food hidden for them and her husband Otto. In January, just before liberation, she had died in Rootje's arms, of exhaustion, starvation and despair. I was sad for Mr. Frank and I hoped Anne and Margot were alive.

A shy, lanky Dutch girl of sixteen called Kea made friends with me. I was glad to have someone my age to talk to in Dutch, and we tried to meet every day for company. Her parents and grandparents had arranged for her to be hidden in Friesland on a farm, but she, too, had been betrayed. She had no news of her family and was totally alone.

During a night of the third week we heard the crack of gunfire near to the camp. Then the boom of artillery. The barrage continued throughout the night as Mutti and I clung to each other in fear under the quilts trying to block out the noise.

When we went down next morning, the street was full of agitated inmates and soldiers. We gradually realized that the Russians had suffered a severe onslaught from the Germans and had lost ground. Our mutual enemy was advancing towards us once more. We were terrified. Having been through all that suffering and survived, we knew that if they were ever to return, they would take bitter revenge and murder us all in cold blood.

Eventually, several Russian officers appeared and calmed us down. They indicated in broken German that they were going to move us back behind the lines to Katowitz, which was in a safer zone. We had to be ready within the hour.

We packed our belongings in a rucksack that Mutti had sewn out of floor-cloths, rolled up our quilts and went down to help Mr. Hirsch. He was still lying in his bunk in great pain. We wanted him to come with us, but he still couldn't move. There were several other very weak men. We hated leaving them behind in danger of being recaptured by Germans. If the Russians could only manage to hold their positions, we knew they would be looked after, but otherwise . . . ?

About 150 men and women assembled in the main square. We were a ragged crowd mostly dressed in striped prison clothes — all with shaven heads — massed together, eager to get out of Auschwitz.

Several lorries rumbled into the square. Russian soldiers let down the flaps and we hauled each other into the back. Rootje and Kea sat with us on the boards, waiting to be driven back to the infamous railway track. Once more we saw cattle trucks waiting for their human cargo, but this time the Russians were taking care of us. This time finally we were on our way to freedom.

20

Katowice

Mutti and I climbed into the train to the sounds of laughter and singing. The atmosphere was so different from our last train journey.

Amid the hustle and bustle we made a little bed for ourselves with one quilt spread out and the other one on top, cosy in our corner ready for a long ride. In the center of the truck was an iron stove burning continually to keep us warm and giving us cooking facilities. And there were to be no more foul-smelling buckets in the corner. This time we were told the train would halt at regular intervals.

The engine slowly pulled away from the most dreadful place on earth. From the Front Line we travelled through liberated Poland. During the day everyone sat quietly round the stove, deep in their own thoughts, hardly daring to hope for more than this quiet comradeship and relative safety. As the train rattled through the countryside, the future was something to be anxious about. The war was still being fought. Few of us were in a fit state to manage on our own, and we wondered what plans the Russians had for us.

Every few hours the train stopped. We all jumped down to relieve ourselves by the track, stretch our legs and breathe in some fresh air. As we gazed around, we witnessed the devastation that the German onslaught and Russian counter-offensive had inflicted upon the land. Time and again we saw deserted, burnt-out villages. But as the train slowed to a halt at small, broken-down stations, hunched shapes would emerge from what seemed like craters in the ground; they were the surviving villagers, peasant women wrapped in shawls and headscarves, laden with baskets of eggs or potatoes which they wanted to sell. None of us had any money, but we held out anything, bits of material, scarves, stockings, socks; anything we offered they seemed glad to have in return. Twice a day when we stopped at a station the Russians gave us soup and bread.

Russian troop trains rolled continuously towards the Front. Whenever we came to a halt near to another stationary train, everybody jumped down to mingle with each other and exchange news from the east and west. We wanted to make contact with people who hadn't been prisoners to find out all we could of the progress of the war.

Some Russian soldiers were little more than children, fifteen or sixteen at the most. A few knew German and spoke to us. Where had we come from? What were conditions like up at the Front? The minute we told them we were Jewish they shook our hands and ran back to their carriages. Then they would proudly bring back one of their Jewish mates and would stand smiling as they watched the immense feeling of kinship flowing between us. The Russian Jews all knew some Yiddish, and they were thrilled and relieved to find Jews who had survived the Holocaust. They seemed to know all about the concentration camps.

Then again, as we stood beside destroyed platforms, Russian soldiers, would pull out photographs from their breast-pockets of parents, brothers or children and ask anxiously if we had seen them . . . somewhere, anywhere.

Some men carried photographs of Stalin which they kissed fervently saying he was our savior, the one to bring us to victory. All the soldiers — strong, earthy men — were fervent communists. They were gripped with enthusiasm and repeated stories of how their own parents or grandparents had been serfs with nothing to look forward to, having to live in hovels like animals, suppressed by the landowners. But now under Stalin they had equal rights and, more important, enough food in their bellies; they dwelt in decent homes and had hope for the future. I was very impressed with their fervor. Their eager faces gave me immense confidence, and I felt certain we would be well protected by men of such conviction.

7 March 1945
US forces cross the Rhine at Remagen

We travelled southeast for almost three weeks, not knowing our final destination until at last, on 25 March, we came to a standstill at a main station which was still intact. It was Katowice, an important Polish coal-mining town where for the first time in many months we entered a built-up area. We were back in civilization.

We took our belongings off the train in good spirits. I noticed Otto Frank getting off the train and pointed him out to Rootje. She nodded and went to walk beside him as we were taken towards the workmen's billets on the outskirts of town. Straw mattresses had been laid out and the soldiers in charge told us to make ourselves comfortable since it would be our home for several days until orders came through telling them what to do with us. We must have been quite a problem for them, but the army seemed to be in control of the situation. Soldiers immediately set up field kitchens in the courtyard for the delicious hot cabbage and potato soup. Lumps of coarse yellow maize bread were available, but it tasted so awful to me that I hardly ate any. Mutti, whose strength was returning only slowly, kept coaxing me to have at least some of my portion.

"All those Russian soldiers eat it," she insisted, "and look how strong and tough they are!"

But I wasn't starving anymore — and I was becoming choosy.

In the afternoons Mutti, Rootje, Kea and I, with a few more of our friends, ventured into town to enjoy the sensation of walking along streets lined with shops. No window displayed much stock, but to us everything seemed the height of luxury. We had no money to buy anything, but we revelled in being part of ordinary life. It wasn't only food that we'd been starved of in Birkenau. We were hungry for normality.

One day, to our great delight, we came upon the local cinema showing an old Austrian film. I was so thrilled and excited that I jumped up and down begging Mutti to ask the cashier if she would allow us to go in. Mutti was extremely reluctant but, seeing my face, she went to the startled-looking girl in the box office and explained that we were a group of freed prisoners from Auschwitz longing to see a film. We looked a sorry sight: stubbly hair, sunken eyes, protruding bones and the oddest assortment of dirty clothes hanging on our bodies. She winced at the sight of us, took pity and agreed to give us free entry. And so a bedraggled group of eager refugees lined up to receive their tickets to escape into the grand illusion of the cinema.

The film had already started. It was dark inside as we

crept to our seats so no one could stare at such oddities as we must have looked. We sank into the plush seats with our eyes glued to the screen. It was a story about Emperor Franz Josef. I recognized the Schoenbrun Palace and gardens where I'd played as a child. The music of Johann Strauss filled the auditorium and during the next two hours I completely forgot the months of misery and torment that we had all endured. It was a total escape from reality.

When it was over, we came out into the darkening street and here I knew we were free at last. The enormity of it staggered me. I was a teenager who had survived the tragedy of Auschwitz, and I supposed I would be going back to normal life, back to school with teachers and schoolfriends, doing everyday things which for many years had been forbidden and out of reach to me. I suddenly felt very scared. How would I be able to cope with it all? It was dark by now and I clung tightly to Mutti's hand, still a child. Although we said nothing, we both thought of Pappy and Heinz. The possibility that they might not have survived loomed in front of us like an ominous shadow.

We stayed in the billets for several days until we were told one morning to prepare to leave. We were to be taken further east since the Russians had to admit that the war was not progressing satisfactorily and the Germans could possibly recapture Katowice.

31 March 1945

Once more we climbed back into a train which headed deep into the Ukraine. Every so often it ground to a halt. Sometimes it would wait several hours to leave the lines free for troop movements. Occasionally it would halt only ten minutes for the convenience of passengers who would jump down the four feet or so to the track to relieve themselves and clamber up again before the train moved off.

On the afternoon of the third day, when the train had already stopped several times, not many took advantage of the latest halt. Mutti got out and was crouching down a few meters from the coach when suddenly the train shuddered and slowly began to move away. Several people were still on the track and were hauled back up. But as Mutti started to run alongside the carriage, she simply didn't have the strength to jump back on and she didn't dare take hold of the hands stretched out to help her. As the train accelerated, she gave up and stopped running. I watched in horror as her lone figure by the side of the track gradually turned into a tiny black dot in the distance. I was hysterical. Rootje and Kea tried to calm me down and reassure me.

"She'll catch the next train."

"She'll join us at the next stop."

"How can she?" I turned on them. "She doesn't know where we're going! *We* don't even know where we're going."

At the next stop the three of us found an officer in charge. He did not understand one word of German, so we had to mime Mutti's plight. It was like a charade. We crouched down making noises, then pretended to try to jump on an imaginary train. We were deadly serious about it, but we must have looked very funny. He thought it was so comical he guffawed with laughter, tears streaming down his face. He patted me on the shoulder to indicate that everything would be alright — but it didn't stop me from worrying or from being angry with Mutti. How could she have been so silly as to leave me alone again? This time it was all her fault.

21

Czernowitz

The journey without Mutti continued eastwards with stops and starts for several more days, and there was no sign of her anywhere.

Apart from my own personal anxiety, the atmosphere in the train was becoming relaxed and even jovial. Some trucks carried Italian prisoners of war who were overjoyed to be out of the fighting. They were full of jokes and songs and sunny charm. Soon everybody was intermingling. Many men and women, starved of each other's company for so long, flirted with each other, and it wasn't long before they were making love in the dark swaying carriages. I was intrigued by the impassioned noises that accompanied the rhythm of the wheels.

All the coupling that was taking place encouraged a man in our carriage to look my way. He tried to creep under my quilt and I didn't like the idea at all. But I understood. He was such a lonely, pathetic figure yearning for love once more, and I didn't want to humiliate him by pushing him away. Luckily for me, I had eaten so many hard-boiled eggs that my constitution complained with a terrible sulphurous odor and much to my relief it seemed to put him off.

Eventually we pulled into the city of Czernowitz, which

had been part of Rumania. The town had once held a large Jewish population protected by the Rumanian government, and rumors of our arrival had preceded us. As we left the station, the streets were lined with Jewish people waving, clapping and coming forward to embrace us and offer small gifts of food or clothes. We were very touched to feel such love and support.

We were marched to an empty school where mattresses filled a large hall which was to be our shelter for a few more days. I was beginning to get used to — and even to enjoy — this nomadic life.

After we had settled ourselves, a small sortie of the more energetic of us went off to explore the town. We walked together in companionable groups of threes and fours, gazing into shops and wandering through residential areas.

Once more the need for toilets began to occupy our minds, so Rootje, Kea and I decided to go into a block of flats, knock on any door and explain the situation. As luck would have it, the door was opened by a motherly Jewish lady who beamed at us and immediately welcomed us in. True to tradition she insisted we stay to have tea in her home. She sat us around her table, and we tucked into home-made cake and sweet tea. Although there was a scarcity of food, her hospitality reminded us of home and made us feel very emotional. We told her of everything we had been through, and when we left, we hugged and kissed her as if we'd known one another all our lives.

As we went out, we noticed a Mezzuzah (the sign of a Jewish household) on her doorpost. From then on we looked for homes that displayed a Mezzuzah. It always worked! Whenever we knocked on the door, we were welcomed with such warmth and love that we enjoyed good cooking and home comforts many times over. These people too had suffered hardship, but they shared what they could with us as honored guests. I felt very pleased I was Jewish.

Everyone we spoke to hated the Germans intensely. We were the few who had been rescued from their clutches, and everybody rejoiced that the Nazis' "Final Solution" had not been final. We felt a great sense of achievement that through all our adversity we had survived.

I WAS ENJOYING MYSELF in Czernowitz even without Mutti. I was experiencing a new kind of independence, and although I worried about her, I fell asleep quite easily on my own.

In the middle of one night the lights in the hall were suddenly switched on and a group of agitated Russian soldiers entered, shouting at us to get up and help. As I woke, I saw them emptying sacks of potatoes into huge piles which had to be peeled immediately. The Russians had sent for reinforcements and many soldiers were about to arrive. They would need to be fed during the night before they left for the Front.

"Not more potato peeling," grumbled some of the older, grumpier women. "We've done enough hard labor," and they flatly refused to get up.

How very ungracious, I thought, feeling ashamed of their attitude.

Kea and I willingly agreed to help with the soup. We more spirited girls would get it done between us. By now we looked upon everything as an adventure and were glad to feel that we could contribute something to the war effort.

We could smell vodka on the breath of the soldiers who organized the potato peeling. They carried buckets of water in relays, and as they did so, they sang traditional Russian songs in deep melodious voices. I was enchanted; alive and excited. When the potato pile had disappeared, they brought in their balalaikas and started to dance. Down on their knees, around on their hands, acrobatic jumping, it was brilliant dancing full of verve and life performed with amazing athletic ability. I had never seen anything like it before. It was a blazing performance as each soldier tumbled in, one after the other, using different kinds of jumps or steps, twirling, whirling around — every one of them an expert dancer. It would have raised the roof in a theatre. We clapped and cheered them on, completely enthralled by their talent and energy. What men these Russians were!

Finally they wanted us to join in. We tried but after one or two feeble attempts we collapsed laughing. I thought I could dance with them — it looked so easy when they performed — but I couldn't manage even one simple step.

In the light of dawn we crawled back exhausted to our mattresses, glowing with excitement at the exuberance of these inspired men. They were genuine, straightforward, uncomplicated and open-hearted, and I loved being with them.

I sank into a deep sleep, but was drawn back to semiconsciousness by the sound of excited voices. Someone was shaking me. I opened my heavy eyelids and there stood Mutti smiling down at me. I had never really doubted our reunion, but strangely my reaction was one of intense anger. How silly of her to have missed all the fun, the good food and company. I sat up and railed at her, getting rid of all my frustration while tears rolled down her cheeks. Then at last we hugged each other and went to sleep reconciled.

22

Mutti's Journey

[Eva's mother takes up the story]

I could hear Eva's screams of panic for a long time after they were muffled by the noise of the train as it accelerated and disappeared into the distance. Standing alone by the track, I stared after it, feeling shocked and angry with myself. Why had I been such a coward? Why hadn't I jumped for the outstretched hands? I felt utterly miserable at being separated from Eva again.

Slowly I picked my way across the sleepers to the bombed station signposted Lemberg. It was quite large and had been repaired in places. I knew it had once been part of Austria, so they ought to speak some German here.

The station hall was crowded with people, mostly peasants. Many lay sleeping and snoring among their baskets and bundles. Behind the counter of the station bar a tired-looking woman was sipping coffee.

"I have lost my daughter," I blurted out in German. "She was on that train. Can you help me?"

The woman looked up at me in surprise, but she must have seen how distressed I was and she came round the counter, sat me down and listened to the whole story.

"Where were you bound for?" she asked.

"I heard someone say Czernowitz," I said, "but I can't be certain."

"Wait here while I go and find out what I can." She disappeared in search of the station master, but my hopes sank when she returned, shaking her head.

"The whole railway is in disorder," she said. "No one knows when the next train will be or where it will go to. Military trains are moving along the lines all the time carrying Russians or liberated prisoners of war, people from the concentration or work camps. You will just have to wait and see."

Well, I will get back to my Eva one way or another, I thought. I was determined that it should be so.

The station master came round and advised me to wait on the platform and to board the first train travelling in the direction of Czernowitz. Meanwhile he offered me some food and coffee to sustain me. It was the start of my experience of the remarkable generosity of people who had suffered all the privations and hardships of war. I was on the receiving end of many simple acts of humanity which touched me deeply and restored my faith and my courage. I could give nothing back except thanks, but it is something I will never forget.

I sat on the platform in the fresh afternoon air and waited. It was very quiet and my thoughts drifted eastwards to Eva. Thank God she was safe. At least she would have Rootje and Kea for company. If it came to the worst, we would meet up in Amsterdam. And then my thoughts turned westwards to Erich and Heinz. If the war ended quickly, they would make their way back home and be waiting for me.

I realized just how lucky I was, remembering Rootje, who was frantic with worry about her daughter Judy in the work camp, and poor Mrs. Frank, who had died of despair in Rootje's arms when her two daughters were transported from

Birkenau. By the time I heard the engine chugging in the distance I felt quite calm and almost ready for adventure.

It was a Russian transport train loaded with trucks and jeeps tied to flat rolling stock. Russian soldiers jumped down as it drew up at the station. I could speak German, French and Dutch fluently. I also had some English but no Russian, so the bar lady came out and acted as interpreter. An officer confirmed that they were going part of the way towards Czernowitz and helped me climb on board and into the front of one of the jeeps. I sat in the driver's seat pretending to drive and we all laughed together. He said something as he jumped in and sat next to me. I imagined he wanted to know where I had come from, so I said, "Auschwitz, but before that Holland."

He beamed and became very excited. *"Ahh, da, Ollandia,"* he exclaimed wielding an imaginary paintbrush in the air. "Rembrandt, Franz Hals, Vermeer!" Then he shook my hand ecstatically.

Just before the train moved off he brought me a loaf of coarse bread, some hard-boiled eggs and − the greatest luxury of all − a piece of boiled meat. I ate it greedily and he seemed pleased. When I pulled off my headscarf to wrap the food in for later and revealed the cropped head of a camp victim, he patted my arm and indicated that I should lie down on the seat to sleep. Then he left me. I slept only fitfully, worried that I would be forgotten and that I would miss my stop.

The train ran on through the night. At dawn it slowed to a halt and a young soldier opened the door of the jeep and signalled for me to get out. As the train moved away, I stood alone on the platform again, not knowing where I was or what to do. There was no one around and everything was silent. Away in the distance I heard a cock crowing followed almost immediately by the far-off chugging of another train coming towards the station.

The noise of the steam engine grew louder as it came into the station and stopped. It was a long-distance train with compartments and a corridor full of soldiers who jumped down to stretch their legs, laughing and joking. I could hardly believe my ears. They were speaking English!

I asked them where they were going. They replied they were English prisoners of war freed by the Russians and on their way to get a ship back home. I told them that I too had been liberated by the Russians, and they listened to my story with astonishment. They had no idea about concentration camps or gas chambers. By the time I had unburdened myself, I was sobbing and insisting that I had to find Eva. One of them had a map, so together they looked up Czernowitz for me. It was not their destination, but they suggested that I travel with them part of the way until I could find another connection. Two of them helped me into the carriage and I sank down gratefully on to the seat.

"I feel so dirty," I apologized. "I've been travelling for days. Is there anywhere on this train I can wash?"

"Now you wait here, my dear," said one soldier, and he sent another to bring back a bowl of hot water, soap and a towel. As the train began to move forward, all the soldiers gallantly left the compartment to wait in the corridor while I made myself clean and fresh again. I was very moved at their courtesy in treating me like a lady once more.

Afterwards I told them my parents and my sister and her family lived in Darwen near Manchester and asked if it was possible to write a letter to be posted in England. Someone produced a pencil and notepad and there in the swaying compartment I wrote the first letter to my family for nearly three years — some two years in hiding and nine months in Auschwitz — telling them that Eva and I had survived. I handed it to a soldier, who folded it carefully into his top pocket and promised to post it the minute he arrived home. I learned some months later that the letter had indeed been sent. Soon afterwards our routes divided, and they left me at a small station called Kolomyya, which was also a former Austrian town. I was sad to part with these English gentlemen.

It was about midday, but everything seemed deserted. The surrounding area was devastated: all the buildings were damaged, and many were derelict. I left the station and wandered around the streets searching for someone to confide in. Only a few old women shuffled past, but then I saw a man with a beard, slightly bent, walking towards a badly bombed house where only the basement and ground floor were intact. I decided to approach him.

"I need help," I said. "Will you help me?"

He looked up at me and his piercing, kindly eyes shone with pity.

"*Shalom.* I'll help if I can," he replied.

He guided me before him into the cellar of what had been his home. In the center stood an old table and chairs; kitchen utensils were stacked on the floor, while bedding and blankets were piled in a corner. His young wife looked worn out but had managed to cook a modest meal on a small fire in one corner. She greeted me with friendly astonishment, insisting that I share their meal with them. As we ate together, we exchanged stories. It happened that they, too, were Jews who had just returned from Russia where they had fled from the Germans. As I told my story of the torment and horror of the concentration camps, they were appalled.

There were to be no trains the following day, and so they

insisted I stay with them, sharing their meager accommodation until they could find out exactly when a train to Russia was due to arrive. On a makeshift bed of blankets and rags, I fell into an exhausted sleep.

The following morning I was taken to another house in a better state of repair where Jewish families were living together for the time being until they could regain their homes and possessions. The news of my arrival had spread and many more came to meet me and listen to my story. Though there were rumors, no one knew exactly what had happened in Auschwitz, and many were openly crying as I told them of the gas chambers and ovens.

I was overwhelmed by the respect with which I was treated. Not only was I offered food — as much as I could eat — but they made a collection to help me on my way. As I sat there with money in my hands, I was overcome with emotion.

I spent the whole day with these good people and returned to the cellar to bed down for the night. At dawn I was awakened by my host, who walked me to the station to join crowds of people from surrounding areas waiting to catch the train. He nodded, pressing my hands as I thanked him.

"God go with you," he said.

He left me to fight my way through the crush of passengers pushing themselves into the carriages. I managed to pull myself up the high steps into a large compartment lined with wooden benches where everyone sat squashed together. They seemed to be farmers or farmhands, animated and cheerful, carrying bottles of vodka from which they regularly took sips. Some held their drink out to me, but I thanked them politely and shook my head. In fact, the odor was so strong it was making me feel faint.

The train rattled along through many stations where passengers dismounted or boarded, no one taking much notice of me, so that I began to feel more alone than ever before. I had no idea where I was going, and it was already dark when we came to a complete halt and everybody got out. Once more I stood on a station platform not knowing what to do next.

A Russian soldier stepped from the shadows stubbing out his cigarette. He glanced at me and I looked anxiously back at him. I pointed to my cropped hair and beckoned to him. He came over and said something in Russian, but we couldn't understand each other — *Russian is such an incomprehensible language,* I thought.

Suddenly fatigue and the strain of the journey made me feel dizzy and faint, and I began to sway and reel backwards. In an instant he was beside me to support me. With his arm round me he led me from the station to a nearby house evidently used as army quarters. We entered an office and several officers nodded as he spoke to them. The Russians tried to question me, each one interrupting the other when they thought they'd found out what I wanted. But it was no use; none of them could understand what I was saying.

Then I had an idea. There was a large wall map behind the main desk, so I searched on it for Czernowitz. I pointed to myself, then to the location and finally to the number on my arm. At last they seemed to understand and agreed with each other.

"Ah Czernowitz, *Da!*"

A soldier was directed to take me to a canteen full of men chatting and smoking. Much to the interest of his mates he sat me down and put tea and bright yellow scrambled egg in front of me. I had never seen anything like it before, but it tasted good. Later I learned that it was powdered egg, a new kind of product the Americans had sent in large quantities to

Russia. The room was filled with smoke. I watched as soldiers tore off small strips of newspaper in which they rolled tobacco, lighting them with great pleasure, inhaling deeply and puffing out huge clouds of smoke.

It can't be very healthy for them, I thought, but they looked the picture of good health with their sturdy frames and ruddy complexions.

My friend sat and waited while I ate and drank thirstily and afterwards indicated that I should follow him down a darkened lane. I had no idea what to expect.

I was led to a tiny village house. He knocked and waited for the door to be opened by a woman whose eyes shone up at him as he explained the situation and indicated what she must do for me. A child of about three clung to her skirt and behind her, by the fireside, sat a wizened old mother in her rocking chair. The woman nodded and smiled as she welcomed me into her home.

I gazed around in amazement. It was the neatest, cleanest room I'd ever been in, just like a doll's house. All the furniture was sparkling clean and pretty. Everywhere, on the two beds in the corners, and on the chairs and stools, there were hand-embroidered cushions in bright colors. The tablecloth was embroidered, there were hand-woven carpets on the wooden floor, pictures of saints on the whitewashed walls and plants on the window sill. A door opened into a neat little kitchen where shining pots and pans hung from hooks. It was so like a gingerbread cottage that I thought I was dreaming.

The woman quickly rearranged the beds. The old mother was tucked into one and I was offered the other, while the woman and little girl made a bed for themselves on the floor. I lay watching the glow of the fire thinking of Eva and when we would be together until I finally fell asleep. I awoke in the middle of the night when the soldier knocked on the door and made signs that I should follow him to the station.

The train was already waiting, full of peasant men and women holding large baskets of food, some with live chickens, on their way to market. He spoke to them about me and I hoped he'd said I should get out at Czernowitz. He stood smiling and waving good-bye to me as the train pulled out of the station. It ran on till daybreak when it came at last to a station signposted CZERNOWITZ, which thankfully I could read as it wasn't written in Russian letters. I had arrived.

The booking office clerk understood German and said there were people from a concentration camp housed in a school nearby.

I walked along the main street as dawn lightened the sky. A group of people were making their way to the station, and I asked them, in German, where the schools were. One woman accompanied me along the road and pointed to a large building. I almost ran towards it, I was so full of joy.

However, I wasn't prepared for the reception I received from Eva. She was asleep on a mattress, and when I woke her up she was very angry with me.

"Where have you been?" she shouted. "I shall never let you get out of the train anymore!"

I was utterly shocked, and I felt tears rolling down my face. When Eva had finally finished yelling at me and I slipped under the quilt beside her, I promised, "We won't ever be separated again." We had been apart for a whole week.

23

Odessa

[Eva's story continued]

13 April 1945
Vienna liberated by the Russians

The snow had disappeared, the sun shone more warmly and trees were beginning to bud. We went every day to the open-air food market where farmers brought in their produce. Most townspeople traded goods with them instead of paying — china or textiles, even small pieces of furniture changed hands for food. Many times the country folk offered me a chicken for my fine leather riding boots, but I refused to give them up just yet. Mutti had been given some money, and we could now buy food if we needed to. We saw and tried something we hadn't had before. It tasted like sour cream, was smooth as velvet and was called *smetena*. It was delicious.

We were having a good time in Czernowitz, but all of us were worried about our relatives. We hoped the Red Cross would contact us as soon as possible with information about them. I had seen Anne's father, Otto Frank, again during the journey from Katowice to Czernowitz standing alone at one of the stops. He looked worn out and sad. Mutti was with me then and asked to be introduced to him. She knew he'd just heard from Rootje that his wife had died, and she felt great pity for him. I took her over and they exchanged polite words, but there was little to console him and he had no interest in anything. He seemed to want to keep himself apart and remain alone with his grief.

Mutti was feeling weak — she was still running a temperature — so in Czernowitz we went to the local hospital. The doctors and nurses were helpful and kind, taking X-rays and examining her thoroughly. We were relieved to learn there was nothing wrong with her lungs, but she was suffering from camp-fever, which would disappear in time under normal conditions.

16 April 1945
US troops reach Nuremburg

News came that we were moving further south. This time after four days' travelling by rail in the usual way, we arrived at Odessa, an important port and resort town on the Black Sea. For us it was another world. As the train entered the town, we could see elegant mansions and villas in lush countryside. The climate was much milder and the foliage was in full leaf.

Only one lorry was available to carry the weakest, so we had to walk to our new home. Soldiers organized the hundred or so of us into groups and said it was about two kilometers away. After an hour, when we began to feel weary, we were coaxed on.

"Just half an hour more."

And after that effort they said, "Come along, just another fifteen minutes."

We were allowed a little rest by the wayside. Then they jollied us up again with "Just another kilometer and we'll be there!"

How long was a Russian kilometer? We tramped on until we had covered at least ten kilometers, and it had taken us four hours!

We were worn out. Every part of us ached as we entered an estate which had once been the summer residence of a Russian prince. To me it was like paradise on earth. The grounds contained several charming, smaller houses which had been used by relatives of the Tsar. Now they were filled to capacity with released prisoners of war, each villa sheltering a different contingent — Australians, Italians, French. But our Jewish group had the privilege of being housed in the palatial main villa. Even so there was no furniture, and we were back to mattresses on the floor, but such an elegant parquet floor! The ceilings were painted with glorious scenes, and the whole decor was ornate and opulent. I had never stayed in such grandeur before, and I was very impressed!

We were warned not to leave the estate or go to town, but we were allowed to wander around and explore the grounds. For the first few days we were so completely exhausted from our journeying that we were happy to comply.

As we relaxed daily in the sun and gazed at the deep blue Black Sea, we began to recover and throw off the yoke of prison mentality. My figure was filling out and my energy came surging back. At one time Mutti had barely been alive. Now she, too, was becoming stronger and looking more attractive.

OUR CURIOSITY EVENTUALLY started to get the better of us. One morning Mutti said, "You know, we'll never have another chance to visit Odessa."

"Are we going to explore it then?" I asked. It seemed a grand idea at the time.

"I don't care too much for regulations anymore," said Mutti, smiling. "So let's go!"

We sauntered off casually through the grounds until we found a suitably secluded spot near to an outside road. Making sure no one was around, we crept through the bushes and started to walk towards the town.

Our breakfast of sweet black tea, maize bread and plum jam was still warm inside us as we walked side by side along country lanes, making for the main road. We could soon hear sounds of traffic and the clanking of an electrified tram travelling towards the city. At the tram stop we waited nervously with the locals. We tried to identify where we were, but all the street signs were in strange Russian writing that we found impossible to read, let alone understand! However, we noted that the villa opposite had an ornate iron gate and several distinct flowering trees, and we told ourselves to count the stops each way.

The tram arrived and we climbed into the crowded carriage, standing room only, swaying into Odessa. It was such a strange odor-filled journey. Every local seemed to have eaten either onions or strange herbs for breakfast!

"What do we do if we're asked for the fare?" I said anxiously.

Mutti was prepared for anything. "We'll just have to speak in Dutch and say we have no money," she said curtly. "What can they do to us?" she shrugged. "They certainly won't shoot us!"

As we drew into the town, the tram became even more crowded, so no ticket collector could get near us and our journey was uneventful. We carefully counted each stop. We agreed to travel for no more than ten stops and then get out.

We alighted in an elegant tree-lined square that had once

been the center of the affluent bourgeoisie. Many villas were now uninhabited and neglected, mainly because of the war and also because the communists did not care to maintain residences of the old regime. Some houses were being used as hospitals with ambulances bringing in wounded soldiers. But the old gardens still sheltered sweet-smelling blossoms and lush semi-tropical plants. Trees bloomed — in glorious contrast to the stark, barren landscape of Auschwitz. The atmosphere of luxury and glory remained, and we were immensely excited. We looked around us, deciding which way to explore.

"We mustn't lose each other ever again," I said, reminding Mutti to stay with me. "And we mustn't lose our way either. Perhaps we should drop little pebbles as markers like Hansel and Gretel."

But Mutti had great confidence that she would know which turning to take on the way back.

We enjoyed our sightseeing for several hours, wandering around Odessa and admiring the beautiful churches with golden-domed cupolas. We appreciated everything we saw. Just to stand and gaze at shop windows, even though practically nothing was available, filled us with pleasure.

Our stomachs told us when it was time to retrace our steps to the square.

"I told you I could find my way back easily," said Mutti.

"But which tram do we catch?" I asked.

The problem was we didn't know! We thought we'd know which it was, but when we were faced with the strange Russian figures, we became very confused.

"This tram is ours," I said, pointing to the first yellow one that pulled up.

"No, it's not," insisted Mutti. So we let it go without us.

"The next one will be ours," she said.

But when it arrived, neither of us was sure. We had lost our confidence completely and were getting very edgy with each other. We couldn't agree which rumbling yellow tram was ours.

I was becoming nervous. If we caught the wrong tram by accident, we would never find our way back to base, and we had no idea what it was called or which side of town it was. How stupid not to know the directions!

As each tram came and went, we stood at the side arguing heatedly.

"We are going to have to trust to chance!" Mutti eventually said in exasperation.

We boarded the very next tram; some letters seemed the same as the original sign. We sank down on a wooden seat as the female conductor approached. Mutti held out her empty palms and drew imaginary bars in the air for prisoners. Then we both pulled up our sleeves and showed her the tattoo marks on our arms. She reacted by talking excitedly and smiling at us, but we had no idea what she was saying so we replied with the only Russian expression we'd picked up *"Ne panya maya"* ("I don't understand"), and she nodded and left us to continue our journey.

We sat glued to the window in case we missed our stop. When we'd counted to nine, we were surprised when the conductress returned and indicated that the next stop was ours. We found out afterwards that dozens of Australians had used this route for several weeks and everyone knew about us!

The Russians had forbidden us to leave the estate, probably for our own good, but we felt sure they wouldn't deny us entrance. With great nonchalance we walked confidently towards the sentry at the gate and pretended not to notice him as we tried to walk past. He wasn't going to have that!

He strode into our path and started shouting incoherent Russian, vehemently shaking his head and pointing to the town. We became scared because he was obviously very cross with us.

He took us both firmly by the arms and walked us over to a large dog kennel beside his gatehouse. Then he knelt us both down, pushed us inside and padlocked the open-barred door. Our two shocked faces stared back at him through the bars.

He bent down to peer at us and then marched off to his gatehouse. Seconds later he returned laughing loudly with two large meatless shinbones and handed them to us through the bars. We were extremely indignant, but there was nothing we could do about it. We were locked in again.

"We only have ourselves to blame," I said. I supposed it was a deserved punishment for breaking the rules. "But I'm tired and hungry," I added miserably.

"Well, I certainly don't relish the thought of having to spend a night in the doghouse!" said Mutti.

We squatted next to each other trying to console ourselves.

"At least our lives aren't in danger," I said.

"If this is the worst punishment we get, then our little excursion was worthwhile, wasn't it?" Mutti said.

"Well worth it!" I agreed.

Our absence from the villa was making Rootje and Kea and our other companions worried. When they found out we were in the doghouse, they all trooped down to see us. They shrieked with laughter at our plight. We all saw the funny side of it, so it became a fairly good-humored punishment!

"But we are *starving!*" I said.

Kea went back to fetch some of the food we stored in our

rooms. We were worldly-wise about food, never letting left-overs return to the kitchen; we were still obsessed by the need to hide food away like squirrels, for who knew what emergencies might arise in the future? We had to stay in the dog kennel for a couple of hours, but we were quite snug and we tucked into bread, cheese and hard-boiled eggs and thought how lucky we were.

21 April 1945
The Red Army reaches the outskirts of Berlin

From now on we decided to be good girls! That was just as well because the following morning we were gathered together to be given some decent clothing. Special tents had been erected on the lawn with field showers, and we were all encouraged to have a good wash. Everyone was in such high spirits that we undressed without too much coaxing – to the men's amusement, including onlooking soldiers. One or two older women were embarrassed and thought it wasn't in good taste, but I didn't mind at all.

After these showers we were handed clean knickers and directed to another tent where a long trestle table was heaped with bras. On a chair by the entrance sat a Russian soldier. It was his dream come true! As each of us passed, he held up both his hands with cupped fingers and had a good squeeze of our bosoms to gauge the size. When he was quite sure of the measurement, he called out to his colleague "small" or "middling"! This gentleman then rummaged round in the pile until he found a suitable cup size which he had great pleasure in fitting on to us, hooking it securely at the back and testing the front with groping palms.

Hilarious fits of laughter and giggling on all sides kept us in good spirits, and I didn't feel at all ashamed or awkward. That was the essence of the character of these men. They were kind, decent people, unaffected and natural, and they did not make us feel immodest. We were all strangely pleased to be wearing bras after such a long time. We felt civilized again.

After that fun we were given olive-green blouses, with hammer-and-sickle motifs on the buttons, and skirts to match. It was the uniform of the women soldiers, and we felt very proud to wear it. We could help ourselves from a heap of shoes if we wanted to replace our worn ones, and I suddenly thought if I could take a pair of shoes to wear I would be able to swap my boots — for a chicken perhaps.

By the afternoon we were all dressed well enough to walk around the park and show ourselves off. Mutti wanted to talk English, so we headed for the liberated Australians. They were a cheerful, optimistic bunch, longing to get back to Australia and their sheep farms. The Red Cross kept them supplied with good things like chocolate and corned beef, which they were always ready to share with us.

To my surprise, one particularly tall, handsome soldier, who looked like a film star in his Aussie uniform and one-sided hat, seemed to like Mutti very much. He kept offering her sweets and other delicacies. He said his name was Bill.

"How about you coming back to my quarters this evening?" he drawled.

"I don't think so," said Mutti, glancing at me.

"You don't have to bring your daughter along," he suggested.

But Mutti did not want such adventures, and when we did visit him I went as chaperone.

They met several times over the next few days, and he began to get very serious. He would sit with Mutti and me outside the villa, planning to take us to his sheep farm, even to the extent of saying he would fetch us from Holland. He wanted to settle down. He owned the farm, there was still a shortage of women in Australia and he felt this was a good opportunity for us to look to the future and resettle there safely.

"You marry me, Fritzi," he said, "and I'll take care of you both."

Mutti was very flattered of course, but she tried to make him understand that she was happily married.

"You may be a widow, Fritzi," he warned, "and then I'll come for you, remember that!"

26 April 1945, 4:40 p.m.
Patrols of US 69th Infantry Division meet forward elements
of Russian 58th Guards Division at Torgau on the Elbe —
Northern and Southern Germany are split in two.

April 1945
Russian shells fall on the Berlin Chancellery

One afternoon some truants returned to say they'd been swimming in the sea. I pestered Mutti to go as well but bathing suits were not on issue, so she sewed me a kind of bikini made from two dishcloths and we went with the next unofficial mixed bathing group. We walked along the avenue until we came to the azure sea stretching beyond golden sands. It was a beautifully warm day and I couldn't wait to put on my tea-towel bikini and run into the water. The men in our party stripped off completely and splashed into the waves with me following after.

Mutti paddled while I swam around feeling exhilarated

and free. She was so moved to see me revel in the pleasure of living once more that on the way back she told me, "It's as if life is coming back to the world and you're still here to enjoy it."

But then we became pensive at the thought of all the others who had not survived, and our longing for Heinz and Pappy grew more than ever. We walked back together, painfully aware that we might never see them again.

28 April 1945
Mussolini and his mistress, Clara Petacci, are executed

30 April 1945
Hitler and Eva Braun commit suicide

24

Repatriation

7 May 1945
Germany surrenders unconditionally

8-9 May 1945
Guns cease firing in Europe

The war was over. The Allies had marched into Berlin. Throughout the estate there was great jubilation. Everyone thanked God, then the Allies, then the Russians and then thanked God again! Vodka was issued freely, so we all got very drunk; there was much dancing and singing and love-making, too.

The Russians organized the best treat that they could for us. At the end of the week a troupe of opera singers, ballet dancers and musicians arrived. They set up a stage in the ballroom of the mansion and gave a magnificent performance. We sat on the floor completely enthralled. It was the first ballet performance I'd ever seen and I'd never imagined anything so pure and wonderful could exist. The audience, which the performers must have found one of the oddest they'd ever played before, rose as one and gave them possibly the greatest ovation they ever received. Our cheers and clapping resounded for ages, and tears of joy streamed down even the most hardened faces. It was an evening I shall never forget!

11 May 1945

My sixteenth birthday! The sun shone the whole day. There was no party but I was so happy. Kea had made me a delicate necklace of shells from the beach, and Bill gave me a huge bar of chocolate. Peace was the best present I could have, apart from news of Pappy and Heinz.

As the days passed, the different groups grew restless. The war was over and we all wanted to return home. In fact, when we went to visit our Aussie friend, Bill, one afternoon, we found the house completely empty. The whole contingent had left without even a farewell!

In one way we were sad, but we realized that efforts were now being made to return us to our own countries and the prospect of being reunited with our families excited us immensely.

We didn't have to wait long. On 19 May the New Zealand troop transport, SS *Monoway,* sailed into Odessa harbor and made preparations to take us on board for repatriation.

Several hundred of us assembled outside the villa to be driven down to the harbor. We were a mixed bunch: men and women who had survived the concentration camps, liberated French and Italian prisoners of war, Dutch and Belgian factory workers that the Germans had commandeered to work in munitions factories, and many voluntary workers from all countries. We had one thing in common — we all wanted to go home.

The great grey hull of the SS *Monoway* lay in the harbor. To us her serene and solid presence seemed a bastion of western democracy and civilization. She was our ship of freedom.

White-uniformed naval officers stood on the deck waiting for us to board. Our only luggage was what we carried in
our arms, and Mutti and I still clung on tightly to our quilts.
We embarked behind Rootje and Kea, and as we stepped on
board we were welcomed by an officer who shook our hands
and called us "Madame." Kea and I were thrilled!

Women were allocated cabins on A and B decks; the men
had to sleep on hammocks lower down. A steward showed us
to our four-berth cabin on B deck, told us to make ourselves
comfortable and said that lunch would be served in the dining room in an hour's time.

Kea and I immediately climbed on to the upper berths and
bounced around. There were soft feather pillows and a luxuri-
ous mattress covered by crisp white sheets and warm blankets. I
tossed down my precious feather quilt for Mutti to pack safely
away in the cupboard. She sat down silently on her bunk. The
four of us were so overwhelmed that we could hardly speak.

We made ourselves look as presentable as possible and
then found our way to the dining room. As we walked
through the doors to the restaurant, we saw that every table
was laid with a spotless white tablecloth, silver-plated cutlery,
shining china and sparkling glasses. It took my breath away.
Only a few weeks ago we had been drinking from chipped tin
mugs. Mutti burst into floods of tears as she took it in. We
were very touched by the way we were being treated as human
beings again.

On each plate was a white roll and a neatly folded white
napkin. The moment we sat down we all grabbed the rolls
and ate them. It was the first white bread we had seen for
years. The stewards watched in astonishment at this peculiar
assortment of passengers who guzzled away without any
manners. But they kindly brought round more rolls. We were

then served with nourishing food in the English style: broth, steak pie and vegetables followed by trifle. Even after a feast like that, when we were all completely full, everyone took a spare roll back to their cabin — just in case!

We came out on deck after lunch to find we were already sailing away on the Black Sea towards Turkey. The sun sparkled on the azure water, and I stood by the rails watching the green land with its white villas recede into a grey blur. I felt sad to be leaving a country that I had come to love. I had hardly had time to wave good-bye to the people to whom I owed the deepest gratitude and for whom I held the warmest regard. I knew I would never forget them.

Despite the nutritious food, served at regular intervals, everybody hid portions of bread, fruit or cheese (anything!) in their cabins until finally the captain announced over the loudspeakers that there was no need to worry — there was plenty of food on board and we only had to ask for it — but please would we not take any more food into the cabins as it was a health risk. We all felt a little foolish and ashamed.

THE TRIP LASTED for seven days. We spent our time sunbathing on the top deck, and many women enjoyed flirting with the officers. We entered the Bosporus, the narrow strait only a few hundred meters wide, with Europe on one side and Asia on the other. The rising hills of Turkey were lush with southern vegetation. In the distance minarets gleamed in the sunlight. The SS *Monoway* sailed on majestically and docked at the harbor at Istanbul.

As it was feared that we might be carriers of infection, we were not allowed to disembark, but the consul generals of all the countries involved boarded the ship and offered to send cables to our relatives on our behalf.

Mutti sat down and wrote to her parents and sister in Lancashire: "We are alive and on our way to Holland. We love you all, Fritzi and Eva."

The Red Cross came on board to collect lists of survivors, and we registered our names. We were in the first group to be released from the East and prayed Pappy and Heinz would be notified that we were safe.

In brilliant weather we left the coast of Turkey to sail through the Dardanelles, across the Mediterranean, to the South of France, and the ship docked in Marseille at noon on 27 May. We crowded on to the decks, pressing ourselves against the rails to watch as two French military bands in full regalia stood to attention and started to play the Marseillaise. It was a wonderful sight; our hearts were full, our eyes misty with emotion. We waved anything we could — mainly stolen napkins! — cheered and shouted until we were hoarse with pleasure.

As we disembarked, the waiting crowd clapped their hands. However, on the boat with us was a group of munitions workers who had volunteered to work for the Germans and who were also being repatriated from the East. When they began to descend the gangway, the crowd went silent and turned their backs. I have always wondered how they knew that these people were not worthy of their applause.

Our group was received by a reception committee sitting at trestle tables on the quayside. They tried to sort out who we were and where we wanted to go. Since not everyone spoke French, there was much confusion and Mutti volunteered to stay and help interpret. This time I had no qualms about being separated from her. Lorries took us to hotels, where we feasted on exotic French food and bottles of wine. I drank at least three glasses, becoming very merry and afterwards very dizzy!

I was still obsessed with food, and when Mutti arrived at the hotel three hours later I shouted, "Why have you been so long? You've missed all the food!" I was so tipsy I could hardly speak.

Mutti simply looked drained and tired.

That same evening we boarded a train with compartments, corridors and proper toilets, and we travelled north towards Paris. Throughout the night we stopped every half an hour or so — at Aix-en-Provence, Avignon, every single station. At some of them gallows had been erected, and straw dummies of Hitler dangled in the breeze. At every station the local population came out to greet us and gave us flowers and bottles of wine. They handed up cakes or cheeses and sticks of French bread, enough for all. Dignitaries of the town with hats and chains stood waiting on platforms while small village bands played through their brassy repertoire with cheerful disregard for anyone trying to sleep. We thought the receptions laid on by the French were magnificent and that they were all for us. It was only after we had passed through Paris and the formal ceremonials became fewer that we realized that returning French prisoners of war had been on the train and the welcome was for them.

Transport was still very disorganized. Throughout the next day we continued our slow progress north, and the train rolled on through Belgium and finally into Holland via Maastricht. Then it stopped. It could go no further. The bridges over the rivers had all been blown up during the Nazi retreat.

About sixty of us were housed in a convent and told we would have to wait until arrangements could be finalized to get us to our homes. There was very little food available, we had no money and we few remaining souls who had suffered the indignities and terrors of the camps felt terribly let down. There was no welcome for us in Holland. We were left to our own devices, and no one seemed to want to help us. The Dutch themselves had suffered great hardship, and they too were exhausted and starved. The plight of Holland and the terrible suffering they had endured contrasted starkly with the plenty we had seen in France. A lorry arrived at the convent two days later. We watched as the occupants, weak, semi-starved survivors of the work camps, climbed down. Suddenly Rootje gave a piercing cry of joy and ran towards a girl who was so thin that she was able to pick her up, cradling her like a baby. Rootje carried her daughter back in her arms sobbing, "Judy, my Judy, my baby." We all wept with happiness for her. It was a miraculous reunion. I just wanted it to be the same for us with Heinz and Pappy.

We had to wait for several days while pontoon bridges were erected over the rivers, then a coach was found to take us to Amsterdam. We drove across country and saw all the damage that the fighting had caused. Here and there flower fields were in bloom and, as we came to the outskirts of the city, we began to feel a rising sense of excitement.

We were taken to the Central Station, and we all hugged and kissed each other good-bye. We promised Rootje and Kea we would keep in touch, but at that moment we could only think about finding out what had happened to our own families.

25

Holland

13 June 1945

At the station city officials took our names and asked where we wanted to go. We had no family in Holland, so we felt we should contact friends who might give us shelter for the night until we got our bearings. We thought of Martin and Rosi Rosenbaum. Although he was Jewish, since she was an Austrian Christian it was just possible they were still living in Amsterdam. We were given money for a taxi fare to their home.

Martin opened the door and recognized us immediately.

"Fritzi Geiringer!" he beamed, embracing first Mutti and then me.

He welcomed us in and said of course we could stay. Then he told us the most extraordinary news. Rosi had just given birth to a son. Who could have imagined it? That seemed to me the greatest miracle of all. Against all the odds, and amid the deprivations and agony of war, a new life had been created. The baby was just three days old, and mother and child were still in hospital.

We visited her that evening. Rosi was very proud of her

son and as amazed at his birth as we were, but she was not feeling very well. She agreed with Martin that Mutti should stay and help look after her and the baby when they came home.

It was a time of austerity. The trees in the streets had been chopped down for fuel, and many wooden doors were missing. There was no gas supply, so we could not use the cooker and had to find fuel for the small woodburning stove. There was precious little to eat. We decided to contact the Reitsmas, who had the keys to the secret store of food we had built up before we went into hiding.

They were overjoyed to see us again. Like Martin and Rosi they had not been deported by the Germans and had survived the hardships of the war. Our secret store of food had saved them in times of near starvation, but now unfortunately there was nothing left. Their son, Floris, had remained in hiding throughout the occupation and had now enrolled at the University of Amsterdam. Both of them looked elderly and frail, but Mrs. Reitsma was excited because she had just been commissioned by the Dutch government to design the postage stamps to commemorate the liberation. She showed us the copper etchings she was working on and promised to give me art lessons when we were settled again.

The day after Rosi returned home with her baby, I heard a knock at the front door and found Otto Frank standing there. His grey suit hung loose on his tall, thin frame, but he looked calm and distinguished.

"We have a visitor," I said as I took him in to see Mutti.

He held out his hand to be introduced to Mutti.

"But we've met already," she said. "On the way to Czernowitz."

He shook his head. His brown eyes were deep-set and sad.

"I don't remember," he said. "I have your address from the list of survivors. I am trying to trace what has happened to Margot and Anne."

He was desolated that he had not yet found them, but he sat and spoke to Mutti for a long time, building up her confidence. She told him she was anxious about Heinz and Pappy and that she was trying to get our apartment back. Other tenants were living in 46 Merwedeplein, but it was still leased in the name of a non-Jewish friend. He said he was staying with Miep Gies and her husband — who had helped to hide the Franks during the war — near the Merwedeplein and would be happy to help in any way if we needed him.

We remained with the Rosenbaums until early July before we could regain possession of our flat. It felt so eerie to walk up the stairs. Inside it was as if the intervening years had not taken place. It was like stepping back in time — everything looked exactly the same. I wandered in and out of the rooms. Our furniture was in the same place, the curtaining and paintwork was unchanged, and when I looked for the spot on my bedroom wall where Pappy had marked my height, it was still there.

I went to the window and looked down into the square. Some children were playing at one end on the tarmac. Later I heard a taxi draw up in the street below and ran to open the door, thinking, *That's Pappy coming home with Heinz.* But it was only a neighbor from across the hall.

Otto Frank visited us from time to time. Mutti was concerned about what to do with me. Should I go to school again or learn a profession? He advised her strongly to send me back to finish my studies at school.

The nightmares started at the end of July. I would wake up screaming. Once I woke up to see Mutti standing by my bed in her dressing gown holding a glass of water for me.

"I can't sleep, Mutti," I said.

"I understand," she said, handing me the glass and sitting on my bed.

"When will Pappy come home?" I asked.

"Tomorrow maybe," she said, stroking my hair and kissing my forehead. Then she tucked me in under my precious quilt and waited on Heinz's bed until I fell asleep.

Epilogue

After matriculating with distinction from the Amsterdam Lyceum, I was persuaded by my mother and Otto Frank to take up photography, and in 1949 I worked as an apprentice in a photographic studio in Amsterdam. But I found it difficult to settle down after my experiences, and I decided to leave Holland for a while.

Otto arranged for me to work in London in a large photo studio in Woburn Square which belonged to an old friend of his. I stayed in a boarding house where I met Zvi Schloss, an economics student from Israel who was working for a stockbroking firm while completing his studies. We were married in Amsterdam in 1952, and Otto was a witness at our wedding.

We set up home in England, where our three daughters were born. Caroline (who was born in 1956) is a London lawyer. Jacky (born in 1958) is a beautician; she is married to Dag Hovelson, a Norwegian, and they live in London with their baby daughter, Lisa (born in 1985). Sylvia, our youngest daughter (born in 1962), also lives in London and works as a journalist.

I continued working as a freelance photographer until

1972, and then I started an antiques business which I still run in northwest London.

Fritzi (Mutti) married Otto in 1953 (making me the post-humous step-sister of Anne Frank) and left Holland for Basel, Switzerland, to join Otto's mother, sister and brother who had remained there during the war. She worked with Otto on the vast correspondence involved in the publication of Anne's *Diary*, but she visited me frequently in England — and still does. Otto came to regard my three girls as his grandchildren. Mutti and Otto shared twenty-seven happily married years until Otto's death in 1980.

Mutti's mother and father (my grandparents) died in England, her father in 1952 and her mother in 1968. My aunt Sylvia (Mutti's sister) died of cancer in 1977, grieving for her youngest son, Jimmy, who was born in England and who died from a brain hemorrhage after a rugby match at the age of twenty-five.

Minni, our cousin who had saved Mutti's life and supported us with her strength and kindness in the hospital block in Birkenau, miraculously survived the death march out of the camp and returned to Prague after the war. Her two teenage sons, Peter and Stephan, had been taken by her sister to Palestine before the war, and she rejoined them there in 1947. She spent many active years caring for new immigrants and the elderly. Her younger son, Stephan, was killed at the age of twenty, fighting in the 1948 War of Independence. She grieved for him until her death in 1984.

Franzi also survived and was liberated in Germany by the Americans. She had contracted tuberculosis and after repatriation to Holland was bedridden for several years under the constant care of devoted friends and her sister, Irene. She finally made a complete recovery, and she lives today in Israel with Irene. She, Mutti and I visit each other frequently.

Rootje lost her husband and, despite finding her daughter Judy, she never entirely recovered from her experiences and frequently suffered from depression. She died in 1984. Judy is happily married with two children. She, Mutti and I became close friends.

Kea lost all her family. She became an art teacher, married an Indonesian and lives in The Hague.

THE FINAL WORDS are for **Heinz** and **Pappy**.

On 8 August 1945 a letter from the Red Cross arrived at our apartment (at about the same time that Otto learned that Anne and Margot had died in Bergen-Belsen). It said that after the forced march from Auschwitz, Heinz had died of exhaustion in April 1945 at Mauthausen.

Pappy, who could not have known that Mutti had been saved or that I would survive the terrible ordeal, probably gave up hope and died three days before the end of the war.

They have no graves. Their names are engraved with hundreds of others on a memorial monument in Amsterdam.

This is also their story.

Postscript by Fritzi Frank

The first time Otto Frank paid Eva and me a visit in Amsterdam after our return from Auschwitz I could see that he was brokenhearted over the loss of his wife, Edith. On the trip from Auschwitz to Odessa he had heard that she had died from exhaustion and starvation in January, just before the arrival of the Russians. But he still hoped, as we did for Erich and Heinz, that his two daughters would return.

When he next came, several weeks later, we had already heard that our dear ones had perished in the Austrian concentration camp of Mauthausen, and he had received the news that Margot and Anne had died from typhoid fever in Bergen-Belsen. We were all acutely depressed. I didn't know how I could carry on. Erich had always organized everything for the family, and now, without him, I felt lost.

On one of Otto's visits he told us that Anne had written a diary while in hiding. Everybody had known about it even though Anne never allowed anyone to read it. She had also written children's stories and would occasionally read one of these to her family and their friends. Miep Gies had found her papers in the Franks' hiding place and had taken them to her office and kept them there. She hadn't read them and intended to give them back to Anne if she returned.

After it was known that she was dead, Miep gave the manuscript to Otto. It took him a long time to read as he found it such an overwhelming emotional experience. When he finished it, he told us that he had discovered that he had not really known his daughter. Although, of course, he was on good terms with her, he had never known anything about her innermost thoughts, her high ideals, her belief in God and her progressive ideas which had surprised him greatly.

He read parts of the manuscript to Eva and me, and Eva told him that she had always had the feeling that Anne was much more mature than she, and that was perhaps the reason why she did not get very close to her.

"If I could meet her today," she said, "we would understand each other much better as I have changed such a lot after all my experiences."

Otto Frank helped to build up the Liberal Jewish community in Amsterdam by becoming one of its board members. He attended the then rather primitive rooms of the synagogue when it was started up, and very often he took me along to the Friday evening services. As we had all lost so many Jewish friends, we liked to meet up with Jewish people and talk with them about their lives during and after the occupation.

He also worked hard at his business, which had to be built up again. He was determined to give those good friends of his who had risked their lives in helping to hide the family the reward of a secure existence again — and in this he succeeded.

When Anne's *Diary* was published in Holland, it became a tremendous success and soon offers from other countries came pouring in. Otto kept me informed about all these events, and I remember that once, when I went to England to visit my parents and my sister, he came along with me to talk to a London publisher. We went by train and boat, and on the trip he gave me more of the material to read.

As time went on, I became his confidante and, in turn, I took my problems to him. I told him about Heinz and how he had been such a gifted boy. At the Lyceum and then at the Jewish School he had proved to be a brilliant student. If he were shown a musical instrument, he could simply pick it up and play it. In hiding he had painted pictures and written poetry — and also taught himself Italian so that he could read Italian books.

Having gone through the same experiences, Otto and I found that we had a lot in common, and he also took an interest in Eva. When he was chosen, as Holland's representative, to attend the conference of the World Union of Progressive Judaism in London, he took Eva along to represent Dutch Jewish Youth.

I often invited him to go to lectures and concerts with me. During Eva's last year at the Lyceum, we decided that she should choose photography as her profession, and she got an apprenticeship at a photographic studio where she would go several afternoons a week. But on the whole Eva was no longer happy living in Holland; it had too many sad memories for her. She decided that she wanted to go to England to perfect her skill in photography.

Now that I was on my own, and as Otto and I grew more and more fond of each other, we decided to marry and move to Switzerland where his family lived. Our wedding was in November 1953 and the marriage, which lasted until Otto's death, was very happy for both of us.

I helped him with his work, answering all the letters he received after Anne's *Diary* had been published in many countries. Together we went to visit Anne Frank Schools and publishers, and we received many young people who had read the *Diary* and wanted to meet Anne's father. Over the years Eva and Zvi had three lovely daughters, whom Otto adopted as his grandchildren. They too loved him dearly.

So, by the tragedy in both our lives, together we found new happiness.

"My Story Is the Story of Anne Frank after Her Diary Ends"

A Fall 2009 Interview with Eva Schloss by the Publisher

Q You write that, after your family left Vienna and settled in a boarding house on the outskirts of Brussels in 1938, you felt that "almost overnight we had become refugees." What made you, as a nine-year-old, feel like a refugee?

A We *had* to leave our country, our home and our family. We moved to a place where I could not speak the language; we lived in two small rooms, and our mother could not run the home; and people were hostile toward us. We had very little money, very few clothes, and we looked, spoke and acted in ways that were obviously different from the local population.

Refugees in Holland

Q Already in early 1934, the Otto Frank family, having left Germany, had moved into a home on the Merwedeplein in Amsterdam. Did you meet the Frank family when you moved there? You speak fondly of your family's life returning to normal in Amsterdam. What was the atmosphere like in that neighborhood when your family arrived?

A We arrived in Amsterdam in February of 1940. We had our own apartment [on the Merwedeplein, the newly developed South Amsterdam neighborhood that had become a magnet for German-Jewish refugees], and we were together again as a family. The Dutch children were very friendly toward me and asked a lot of questions about life in Austria, so I began to feel more important.

Anne Frank and I knew each other for about two and a half years on the Merwedeplein. She was just a month younger than I was. We saw each other every day after school because the children of the neighborhood would play together outside on the street. But Anne was more advanced and sophisticated than I was. She was quite a talker, and she liked telling her stories and being the center of attention. I was more shy at that time. Anne loved parties and she liked having a boyfriend; in fact, she was quite a flirt. I had a brother, so for me being around a boy was nothing special. Heinz, my brother, would often do homework with Anne's sister, Margot.

In that district of Amsterdam there were also many people who spoke German, so I did not feel so different anymore.

Q You also speak fondly of your early encounters with Otto Frank. Did you feel like you had a special bond because of Otto's kindness to you — even at eleven years old?

A I got to know Otto Frank when I would go over to the Franks' apartment to play with their cat. Otto was much older than my own father — closer to my grandfather's age, in my mind. I had had a very close relationship with my grandfather in Vienna, and I missed him terribly. I sort of related to Otto as I would to my grandfather, but he, for his part, was kind to everybody.

Q In what ways did everything change in Amsterdam — and what were some things a young girl felt — as of May 10, 1940, when the German occupation of the Netherlands began? How much did your parents talk with you about the dangers after that date?

A We had already experienced the Nazis in Vienna, so this was a repeat of what we had seen there. We knew how they were treating the Jews in Germany and Austria, so we already knew what to expect. The Dutch Jews were less scared: they did not want to believe that they would be treated differently than Dutch Christians were treated. For us children, initially, the most difficult things were that we could not go with our non-Jewish friends to the swimming pool, the cinema, to clubs, and later not even to school. Later, when people were actually arrested on the street — and some people simply disappeared — it became very scary to even go out onto the street to shop. But our parents didn't really talk about it until we were forced into hiding.

Two Years in Hiding

Q Many Amsterdam Jews had gone into hiding by July 1942. What event(s) influenced that decision on their part? The Franks and van Pelses had eight people hiding together, so why did you and Mutti have to be separated from Heinz and Pappy?

A My father and Otto Frank decided to go into hiding in July of 1942, when about ten thousand young people received deportation orders — to be conscripted into labor camps. My older brother, Heinz, received that notice, as did Anne Frank's older sister, Margot. That's when our parents decided that it was time to disappear. But many other Jews did not go into hiding, because of lack of money, because they thought they had connections, because they did not believe they would be killed — for any number of reasons. As a result of this false confidence, many Jews were deported — to concentration camps and death camps.

We depended on brave Dutch people who were risking their lives to help Jewish people. Most people in the city lived in small apartments, so there was not enough room — and it was too risky — to take in a whole family. A family of four people would have been too many. Don't forget that the Franks and van Pelses were living in the attic above the office of their business, and there were few searches there. There were sometimes more people hiding together on farms (as Heinz and Pappy were) simply because there was more room on the farms.

When we were in hiding there was very little food; everything was rationed. We did know something of what was going on in the world because we listened to radio broadcasts, and we thus also realized that some friends had disappeared. The nights were very worrisome due to the searches; but during the daytime, life was monotonous because there was little for us to occupy ourselves with. And, of course, I never expected that it would last for two years — two years of my early childhood! Basically, I had to sit still for two years, and I had no company. I mean, I loved my mother, but she wasn't like another child I could have fun with.

Q The Nazis, of course, realized that many Jewish people had simply disappeared. How often did they come looking for hidden Jews? And how often was it necessary for you to move?

A There were house searches about every week. Before we were arrested, Mutti and I had to change hiding places seven times in two years. I think that my father and brother moved about four times in that period. We had to change hiding places so often because, after several months of the weekly checks by the Nazis, those who were hiding us would become very nervous: obviously, they thought that one day the Nazis would find us. There was so much tension in the air that they would eventually say, "We're sorry, you know . . . but you are going to have to find a different place to hide."

Mutti and I were not living with Pappy and Heinz during that time, but we were able to visit them sometimes because we could actually travel on trains: we did not look Jewish with our blond hair, and we had false papers as well. But one time when we went to visit them, we were followed from our hiding place, and it was a trap. We had been betrayed by a Dutch nurse who was a double agent. So all four of us were arrested at the same time, and we were taken to headquarters to be interrogated.

The Birkenau Concentration Camp

Q You write that your mother was separated from you at Birkenau for three months. How and why did that happen? And how were you and she reunited?

A Yes, my mother was selected by Mengele himself to be gassed. For three months I thought she was dead, and that was really my worst time in the camp. But she was saved by our cousin Minni, who worked in the sick ward and stealthily kept Mutti alive there. Mutti just kept getting sicker and weaker, but Minni kept her in the sick ward.

In January 1945, when the Germans started to realize that the Russians were approaching, the regime in the camp was not so strict anymore, and things abruptly reversed. I was able to move — via some tricks — to another part of the camp, where I was reunited with my mother. All of this was a real miracle!

Now, suddenly, *I* was looking after Mutti — and I grew up at that very point. I felt that this was a very important moment for me. What I knew at that moment was this: She is not able to look after me anymore. I need to look after *her.*

Q A very small number of Jews actually survived the concentration camps. But you and Mutti, Otto, Franzi and Minni did survive. What did you and they have that enabled you all to survive?

A Luck . . . luck . . . and more luck. Our family was deported to Birkenau in May 1944, and the Frank family was deported in August 1944. Had we been deported to the camps earlier, we would probably never have survived. Also, we did not have to wait until the end of the war to be liberated, because we were free as of January 1945, when the Russians came. As it was, Anne and Margot Frank died of typhus; my brother died of exhaustion during the forced marches — and probably my father, too. Of course, my father, in addition to knowing that his son had died, thought that his wife had died, and did not know about his daughter (me) — so he had probably given up all hope.

Millions of other people did not survive the camps and the death marches, and it's good for folks to know about this because many do not realize what it meant. People will often ask me, "Did you make friends? What did you do for entertainment? Did you have free time?" These questions betray a profound ignorance of what a concentration camp was like. You know, there was just absolutely nothing. We were waiting for death. Anyone who died *before* being summoned to be gassed was just one less person they had to kill. So they made life as difficult and terrible as possible. We had to get up at 4:00 a.m., which was roll call time; and we didn't get to bed until 8:00 or 9:00 at night. Of course, we didn't have watches, so we never knew exactly what time it was. We were simply always dead tired.

At one point I was forced to carry big rocks from one place to another. My mother told me that when she saw me walking in front of her burdened down with rocks — and finding it very difficult — she just wept that her little girl had to do this terrible work, and she could do nothing about it.

Many died of typhus, dysentery or cholera; and thousands died simply from exhaustion and from lack of food. During the winter, there was a huge amount of snow that was never cleared, and there was no heat in the barracks. The food was never warm. When we slept at night, there was never a covering or any more clothes.

But Mutti and I had each other for much of the time; and we also had Minni and Franzi. When we were in Birkenau, many times I felt that my life was threatened, but I never gave up hope. If you thought for one second that you had no hope, you would soon be dead. So we remained too stubborn to give up hope.

Liberation and Postwar Life

Q You write with admiration and warmth about the Russians who liberated Auschwitz-Birkenau. What did you think of the Communist revolution and the atrocities under Stalin when you learned about them?

A We did not know what Stalin had done to his people at that time. Russia was very isolated, and news did not travel as easily and as fast then as it does now. But all the Russian soldiers spoke of Stalin with great love and affection. Of course, I was in contact only with soldiers and just a very few of the Russian civilian population, and the people I did know were generous, brave and wonderful people.

Q Though you refer to events in your story sometimes as "answers to prayer," you describe your family as "High Holy Days" Jews rather than fully observant or devout. How did your experiences during the war and your imprisonment change your faith?

A I think that this is an important question because many, many people did lose their belief in the existence of God — including me. The only thing we could do unhindered in the camp was silently pray for life to return to normal, in my case for Pappy and Heinz to return. Unfortunately, those prayers seemed to be of no avail. So when I first came out of the camps, I was an atheist. But after the war was over and as time moved on, and I saw the wonderful things around me in nature, in the births of my children and grandchildren — well, I thought it's all so wonderful, so marvelous, that there must be a higher being. I thought that life would be meaningless if I were just to live it out and say, "That's it!"

I questioned whether it was God's responsibility that the death camps existed. And I decided, no, it's our responsibility. God gave us free will, and it is up to us to choose between good and evil. When I reflected more on my whole experience and my survival, I became a believer again, a very committed Jew. I realized that we did survive — against all odds. No Jew was supposed to have survived. But our race and people did survive! I believe that we have a special task to fulfill in this world, which is till now a mystery. But one day God will show his face again.

Q You say that, even with the Russian liberation of Auschwitz-Birkenau imminent, many women you knew were dying daily of starvation and disease (not to mention exposure to the cold). And Mutti was also ill enough to be in the sick ward. How close do you believe you and Mutti came to not making it out of Birkenau alive?

A Mutti was very, very weak: she was running a temperature and was extremely undernourished. I had very bad frostbite on my feet. I believe that in a matter of a week or so, the toes would have gone septic and I would not have been able to walk. That alone would have been grounds for me to be killed if the camp would still have been in operation under the Germans. In fact, if the Russians would have come a week later, I don't believe that either Mutti or I would have been alive to greet them.

But when the Russians did come in January 1945, we did not really accept the fact that we were liberated, because the war was not over — in fact, it went on for five more months. We were with the Russians for much of that time, and they did share whatever little they had with us. But we were still sleeping on the floor and were still traveling in cattle cars, and we saw terrible devastation. Many people even died after liberation because, when they got food, their bodies could not digest it and they died from overeating. We were very weak, and we were very anxious about what had happened to our families. So there was not really the rejoicing in liberation that you might expect.

Q Did you have any lingering health problems as a result of your time in Birkenau?

A For many years I had trouble with my toes, and I had digestive problems as well. After we got back, I was on a simple diet of pasta, rice and mashed potatoes — food like that — because I could not digest heavier, more complex foods for many years. My mother was quite ill for many months after the liberation. But the body is something very wonderful. My mother lived to be 93, and Otto Frank was 91 when he died. I am over 80. I'm still good on my feet and continue to be quite active.

Q Upon your return from Russia after liberation — via France — how did Amsterdam, the home to which you returned, compare with France?

A The south of France and many other parts of Europe had already been liberated months before Holland was freed. The Germans kept Holland occupied until the end of the war. The last winter of that occupation was called the Hunger Winter: thousands of Dutch people died of starvation. In France we were given food and wine and all kinds of things that were pure luxuries to us. But in Amsterdam, when we returned, there was nothing to eat and no fuel. There was only a great deal of misery.

Q After Auschwitz-Birkenau were liberated, and you did not find Pappy and Heinz, where did you think they had been taken? And then, by the time you and Mutti were back in

Amsterdam, Otto Frank was also there and he was likewise waiting for any word about Margot and Anne.

A When we heard that Pappy and Heinz were still alive in January 1945, but that they were on a transport to take them back inside Germany, we were hopeful that the war would soon end and that they would still be alive. Only later, after the war was over, did we hear that those transports were called "death marches." Thousands of people perished on those forced marches. Near the beginning of July — this was now two months after the war in Europe had ended — after we had moved back into our apartment in Amsterdam, we heard from the Red Cross about the deaths of Pappy and Heinz.

Otto had learned of his wife's death on the trip to Odessa that those of us who had been liberated from Auschwitz had taken. But it was not until we were all back in Amsterdam that he learned of the death of his daughters. Otto had tracked down a woman who had been at Bergen-Belsen when Anne and Margot died. When Otto first came to our house, it was to tell us that terrible news. He was just devastated.

Otto returned a few days later with a parcel under his arm; he opened it very carefully and lovingly. It was Anne's diary, and I remember that scene very clearly. Otto could only read a couple passages from it before bursting into tears. It was too emotional an experience for him. But the diary was really a lifeline for him, because before that he was in a desperate state; but through the diary, he found that Anne was still really with him.

Q You have said that you were very bitter and full of hatred for twenty years after your survival of the camps. How were you able to break that cycle and rebuild your life?

A It took a very, very long time for me to get over my depression, my hatred of the Nazis and my suspicion of people in general. Otto Frank started coming to our home very often, to talk with Fritzi (Mutti) and me, and to help my mother with me. I was a very sad teenager, very difficult. I couldn't live an ordinary life — couldn't make friends — and he was a childless father, a man who had lost everything that was dear to him in his life. So we all became very close.

Otto was amazing. Even though he had lost everything he held dear, there was no bitterness or vengefulness in Otto — not even toward the Germans. He was very proud of being a German. "Well," he said, "after all, not all Germans are bad. *We* are also Germans. You can't condemn them forever. That would be like Hitler — condemning a whole people." I found that extraordinary. So Otto — with his uplifting attitude and frequent visits to our home — outlined a happier life for me in the future.

After finishing school, I left for England for a year, and I suppose my mother and Otto became even closer. They were married in 1953, a year after I got married, and were together for twenty-seven years — until Otto's death in 1980. And I've never seen a happier couple than those two. They really devoted their lives to the publication and aftermath of *Anne Frank: The Diary of a Young Girl* (it was made into a play and a movie and was translated into seventy languages). When my mother died in 1998, I found copies of thirty thousand letters that they had written to people all over the world. That really was their life.

Q What happened to the people who helped to hide Jewish people like you?

A In general, those people were also arrested and sent to

concentration camps — not in Germany or Poland, but in the Netherlands and Belgium (where there were concentration camps as well). People were not killed there, but the living conditions were so bad and there were so many kinds of diseases, that if you were there for any length of time, you sometimes starved to death or died of a disease. Sometimes they shot Resistance workers and those who hid Jews. People really had to have moral courage to hide the fugitives. Luckily for us, there were many Dutch people who did help us.

Q Soon after the war, you wanted to tell your story of the Holocaust, but people did not want to talk about or hear about the war. Was that true in the UK as well as on the Continent, and how long did that attitude continue?

A I wanted to tell people about my suffering. I wanted people to feel sorry for me, but they just said, "We know it was dreadful. We have all suffered tremendously. Just try to carry on with your life." That was, of course, easier said than done. This was certainly the case in England and the Netherlands; and I believe it was very much the case in Germany as well. That country was occupied after the war, and it was in ruins, and nobody wanted to talk about Germany's guilt. After maybe ten years, when people started to ask questions, those of us who were survivors didn't want to talk about it anymore. We had suppressed it.

Q Then, more than forty years after the war and Holocaust had ended, you decided to tell your story — in the late 1980s. Why?

A I was inspired to tell my story when I realized that the world had not learned what really happened, and I felt it necessary to get down in writing what happened to me so that others would learn the truth from it. After the war, people said, "We have learned our lesson — there will never be another Auschwitz." But by the 1970s and '80s there was plenty of prejudice and hatred again, along with wars, genocide, and "ethnic cleansing." In addition, some people at that time started to deny that the Holocaust had ever happened. So, in reaction to such vile propaganda, many survivors were ready to talk about their experiences of the Holocaust. We decided that it was our responsibility to educate young people about the dangers of discrimination, prejudice and violence against a singled-out group of people.

Anne's wish was to live on after she died. I think that, in a remarkable way, she has — through the publication of the *Diary* and its tremendous success. Wherever you go, you only have to mention her name and everyone knows about her life. But my mother and I always felt that Heinz and those other 1.5 million Jewish children who perished have been more or less forgotten. My brother was not even eighteen when he died, and he was definitely a special person — sensitive, artistic, and very talented — but basically forgotten by the world. As a survivor, I feel that I owe it to him to share something of our family — my close relationships with my father and him and the love we had — with readers all over the world.

Q What do you believe children, teens, and adults can learn by reading *Eva's Story*? And what can we do, in these early years of the twenty-first century, to assure that "ethnic cleansing" or another Holocaust will not happen again?

A I have told people in England and America that my story is Anne Frank's story after her famous *Diary* ends. It is thus a sequel to Anne's *Diary,* the story she could not tell because she died, but that I could tell because I survived. In telling the story of a girl of Anne's same age and one of her playmates in Amsterdam, my story shows what would have happened to Anne — and did happen to the rest of us — after we were all betrayed and arrested.

I wrote my story in part to commemorate the lives of twelve million people all over Europe who were victims of the Nazi regime. Whole families disappeared, and it is important for us to remember those people whose legacy disappeared from the face of the earth. But not only that. Unfortunately, we have again experienced genocide around the world at the dawn of the twenty-first century: religious ignorance, hatred and discrimination that has been practiced against minority groups among us. I believe with all my heart that this, most definitely, must stop.

We need to learn to live with each other in harmony, to accept each other for who and what we are. We must learn the lesson that human differences actually enrich our lives. We should not be afraid of people who are different from us, but we need to embrace their faiths and ways of life so that we can give our children and future generations a safer life to live. We all have to work at this, and I hope that we can teach our following generations to have moral courage: both to exercise tolerance as they grow up, and also to speak up and stand up against intolerance, racial prejudice and systematic discrimination when they see it.

I believe that my story also illustrates the importance of family-based values, which is a significant lesson for young readers to learn. Without the love of my parents and my brother, I would not have survived.

Q Eva, you have passages in your memoir (for example, pp. 128-29) about the horrors of a fifteen-year-old girl (you) carrying the dead bodies out of the women's barracks ("Bodies stared at me open-eyed from stiffened mounds of dead flesh and bones. Here were faces I had come to know and respect"). This first-person witness and emotional devastation is much more horrific than anything in Anne Frank's *Diary.* To be sure, Anne deals with everyone's fear of being arrested; but her narrative is also about the banality of life that you all lived while hiding in attics. And, of course, Anne's *Diary* stops at the moment her family was arrested in Amsterdam. In a very recent book, *Anne Frank: The Life, the Book, the Afterlife* (2009), Francine Prose points out that, despite Otto Frank's best efforts, the American stage version (1955) and movie version (1959) of the *Diary* succeeded in infantilizing Anne and making her statement at the end of the *Diary* ("I believe that people are good at heart . . .") a kind of Pollyanna-ish ending for feel-good American audiences, thus not forcing anyone to look into the heart of darkness that was the Holocaust.

And, despite the much more graphic descriptions — both physical and psychological — of violence in your narrative, the very last sentence of your book (your mother's postscript) also shows a kind of optimism: "So, by the tragedy in both our lives, together we [she and Otto Frank] found new happiness." Do you believe that readers of your story should feel optimistic about how humans can live together in peace on this planet or that they should feel pessimistic about the fact that humans always seem to find ways to annihilate each other? Or, after reading your book, should we find ourselves at the paradoxical ambivalence where those two seemingly op-posite perceptions confront each other?

A Two observations about your complex question. I think that, in the 1950s, the American public (perhaps people in Europe as well) was not ready to see a play or film about Anne Frank in which more of the horrors of the Holo-caust would have been described. My second observation is this: I am basically an optimist. I think that there will always be conflicts and even wars, but we are trying more than ever to negotiate and to find ways to eliminate con-flicts. Also, in the long run, as there is a good deal more intermarriage among the different races, racism will be greatly diminished. I believe that there will always be evil people around, but the decent people will be in a large majority. And everyone must have hope that things will get better; otherwise, we might as well give up. And that is clearly something we should never be prepared to do.

Discussion Questions

1. *Eva's Story* weaves world events in bold type throughout the narrative. Research one or two of the events, such as Kristallnacht (p. 12) or the Battle of the Bulge (p. 121). What effect does the inclusion of these events create? How do these events contrast with or inform Eva's experience at that point in the narrative?

2. The United States Holocaust Museum summarizes the Holocaust as "the systematic, bureaucratic, state-sponsored persecution and murder of approximately six million Jews by the Nazi regime and its collaborators." Nazi forces also killed an estimated eleven million others, including Roma (Gypsies), those with disabilities, Slavic peoples (especially Poles and Russians), Communists, Socialists, Jehovah's Witnesses, and homosexuals. How do personal narratives like *Eva's Story* help us make meaning of large statistics like these?

3. When a woman is hanged inside the camp, Eva says that "none of us really saw the hanging. We were forced to look — but we did not see" (p. 78). She uses similar

language when describing the farmers "turning the other away" (p. 79) when the prisoners march by on their way to "Canada." How is the prisoners' not seeing the hanging different from the farmers' refusal to see the prisoners?

4. Why do small acts of resistance (such as the shower incident, pp. 106-108) matter so much to Eva and her fellow prisoners?

5. Why do you think *Eva's Story* continues after the liberation of the camps, going on describe much of Eva's postwar life?

6. Why do Eva, her family, and those around them value "normalcy" so highly? Discuss what normal school activities, clothes, etc., meant as a refugee, as a prisoner, or as a recently freed survivor. How does this relate to the survivors' response to luxuries (wine, feather pillows, etc.) on the SS *Monoway*?

7. Eva writes that after she and the other survivors walk out of the movie theater in Katowice, she knew they "were free at last" (p. 166). Why do you think she has that realization at this particular moment? And why do you think she feels scared by the idea of going back to regular life?

8. What moments or conversations throughout the book surprised you? Does your surprise reveal any assumptions you might have had?

9. If you've read Anne Frank's *Diary of a Young Girl*, you might have a different perception of the stylish teenager Eva describes. How is the Anne Frank of Eva's memory

different from the one in the *Diary*? What might this suggest about our perceptions of those who have died, especially those who died in the Holocaust?

10. Think about other Holocaust-era stories you might have read or watched, including Anne Frank's *Diary of a Young Girl*. How do they differ from *Eva's Story*? What similarities do they share? Consider both content and perspective.

11. What can be learned from the choices of the Reitsmas, Mrs. De Bruin, and others who hid Jews? How does Mrs. De Bruin's blackmail of Mutti (pp. 36–37) complicate our interpretation of her actions?

12. "I believe there will always be evil people around, but the decent people will be in a large majority," Eva says at the end of the interview (p. 226). Do you agree or disagree with this statement? Why?

13. *Eva's Story* explores a number of themes, including community (pp. 163, 176, etc.), confidence/faith (pp. 47, 164, 215–216, etc.), and studying or creating art amid conflict (pp. 33, 171, etc.). Pick one of these themes, or another of your own choosing, and discuss its significance throughout the memoir.

Recommended Resources for Further Research and Discussion

- **116 Cameras, *New York Times*:** This fifteen-minute documentary follows Eva as she records her story for New Dimensions in Testimony. The New Dimensions project hopes to facilitate three-dimensional conversations with Holocaust survivors for decades to come.

- **United States Holocaust Memorial Museum:** The Washington, D.C., museum website includes online exhibits, the First Person podcast series, and helpful guidelines for discussing the Holocaust.

- **Gale Opposing Viewpoints in Context Database, "Genocide" page** (available through many public and academic libraries): This database collects a variety of Holocaust-related resources, including topic overviews on anti-Semitism and viewpoint essays on preventing further genocides.

- **History Unfolded: US Newspapers and the Holocaust:** Through this growing collection of contemporaneous articles, readers can assess US responses to the growing persecution of Jews during the Holocaust.

The database can be searched for major events and locations, including those mentioned in *Eva's Story*, and organizers encourage visitors to participate in gathering articles from their own local newspapers.

- Many North American and international cities host a Holocaust museum or memorial, including the National Holocaust Monument in Ottawa, Ontario; the New England Holocaust Memorial in Boston, Massachusetts; and the Judenplatz Holocaust Memorial in Vienna, Austria. Check with your local government to locate one in your city, state, or province.